PRESENTED TO:

_____

FROM:

_____

DATE:

Other books by Michele Howe

*Prayers for Homeschool Moms*
*Prayers to Nourish a Woman's Heart*
*Pilgrim Prayers for Single Mothers*
*Going It Alone: Meeting the Challenges
    of Being a Single Mom*
*Successful Single Moms*

# Prayers
## of
# Comfort and Strength

# Prayers

## of

# Comfort and Strength

## Michele Howe

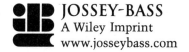

JOSSEY-BASS
A Wiley Imprint
www.josseybass.com

Published by Jossey-Bass
A Wiley Imprint
989 Market Street, San Francisco, CA 94103-1741   www.josseybass.com

Jossey-Bass books and products are available through most bookstores. To contact Jossey-Bass directly call our Customer Care Department within the U.S. at 800-956-7739, outside the U.S. at 317-572-3986, or fax 317-572-4002.

Jossey-Bass also publishes its books in a variety of electronic formats. Some content that appears in print may not be available in electronic books.

Unless otherwise noted, the Scripture quotations contained herein are from the New American Standard Bible®, Copyright © 1960, 1962, 1963, 1968, 1971, 1973, 1975, 1977, 1995 by The Lockman Foundation. Used by permission. (www.Lockman.org)

**Library of Congress Cataloging-in-Publication Data**
Prayers of comfort and strength / Michele Howe.—1st ed.
p. cm.
Includes bibliographical references.
ISBN 0-7879-6769-6 (alk. paper)
1. Christian women—Prayer-books and devotions—English. I. Title.
BV4844.P72 2003
242—dc21                    2003007630

FIRST EDITION
*HB Printing*   10 9 8 7 6 5 4 3 2 1

# Contents

To Maddie,
my friend for all seasons

# A Note to the Reader

Before you begin reading the stories of the many courageous women whose lives are depicted in this book, let me offer a brief word. Unlike some magazines or books that you might read in which the main character endures a terrible ordeal but by the story's completion a Cinderella ending is apparent to all, this collection may not provide the same immediate "feel good" emotions. Yet my hope is that in the same way that our lives sometimes unfold we all realize that prayer is the starting point for solving a problem, whether it is one of overcoming grief, finding strength, or coping with challenges. The hope is in the prayer, not the magic ending of a story, because the moment at which we accept our need for divine intervention is exactly when significant, life-changing resources become available to us—despite any dire circumstances we may face. Our call then is to remember from where we will receive the help we need and go directly, unhesitatingly to the Source.

*Is anyone among you suffering? Let him pray.*
—JAMES 5:13A.

# Acknowledgments

As the years go by, I am astounded by the exponential increase of painful life events those I encounter must endure. Friends, family, and acquaintances all seem to face increasingly difficult challenges. I used to wonder about this. Does advancing age necessarily imply more highly concentrated seasons of suffering? Admittedly, life does get more complicated, but right alongside the hardships are some significant counterparts; namely, wisdom, understanding, vision, insight, maturity, experience, and, perhaps most important, joy. I can't say that I always like what I see happening around me, but as I look and listen to those who are walking ahead of me, I find comfort in their company. This selection of stories is written in honor of those whose lives have been dramatically affected by an outpouring of life's downturns and upsets. Yet their overall message is one of hope, for with God there is hope. My prayer is that each of these stories will bring you renewed resolve to see all of life's trials through the lens of God's redemptive power and purpose.

Once again, I am grateful to be numbered among the Jossey-Bass authors. It has been a whirlwind year of writing and rewriting and I wouldn't trade it for any other experience. That fact alone says much for my outstanding editor,

Mark Kerr, who has demonstrated his expertise and graciousness in countless ways. Thank you, friend. And as every writer and reader knows, producing books is a group endeavor, the product of many skillful professionals. So I also want to thank Andrea Flint, production editor; Sandy Siegle, marketing manager; and Paula Goldstein, director, creative services. It has been such a pleasure working with you and your teams. Many grateful thanks.

# Prayers
## of
# Comfort and Strength

# PART ONE

## Too Much to Handle

*O*verwhelmed and undone by events that pile one burden upon another, weary women sometimes feel good cause to give up. Nothing looks more appealing than taking a permanent vacation from life. But for most women the thought of really giving up is unthinkable—there is too much at stake. Children, grandchildren, friends, neighbors, and work associates all depend upon the stalwart affection and constant support of these committed individuals. Instead of buckling under a load of despair, these women look to God to supply their needs so they in turn may supply the needs of others. A high calling indeed.

# I

# Penny Pinch

Gwen counted out the change in her purse, almost six dollars and some odd pennies. Enough, she thought with relief. "Here's the money you need for today's lunches kids." Handing off her final cash reserve, Gwen experienced both a rash sense of relief and anxiety. *It's only Tuesday and I just know someone's going to need more money before Friday.* Shaking her head, Gwen turned her thoughts to meal planning. *Let's see,* she pondered, *what inexpensive meals can I turn out until the paycheck comes in?* Some minutes later, Gwen felt a tad more at ease. *That's one more task out of the way,* she thought. *Now on to the difficult stuff,* Gwen reached for the newspaper and took out her red pen, armed and ready to circle any possible job openings. *It was so aggravating, this issue of budgeting,* Gwen decided as she looked down column after column of advertisements. She didn't want to get a job working full-time. Gwen was happy working from her home selling personal care products and further supplementing the family's income by occasionally filling in as the church secretary. But the little she brought in hadn't made a dent in their debt. Gwen's husband finally told her that for at least the next year, she'd need to get a job. "Doing what?" Gwen asked. "Anything," the curt reply.

So today was D day and Gwen was determined not to allow her fear of the unknown to hinder her from this job search. Though she'd been diligent to cut costs in the past month or so, Gwen admitted that both she and her husband had been living far above their means for the last several years. In the back of her mind, Gwen had been trying to ignore the niggling little voice that continually cautioned her to pare back and live more frugally. But she hadn't listened and now she was paying the price.

Gwen worked her way through the entire ten-page listing and circled seven possibilities. Tearing the ads out, she wanted to cry again. How would getting a full-time position away from home change their lives? Gwen wondered. Suddenly overcome by the immense transition they would be facing, Gwen sat back in her chair, closed her eyes, and cried out to God for some small measure of strength and peace of mind.

*You are not restrained by us, but you are restrained in your own affections.*
—2 CORINTHIANS 6:12

*Dear Lord, upon waking up this morning I was suddenly shaken with the realization that today was it, no longer could I make excuses for not following through on this task. Oh, how I wanted to climb back under the covers and sleep the day away. But it was no use. My poor choices have finally caught up with me. Now I must tackle the difficult work of digging myself out of the trenches of debt we've accumulated. Lord, this is not going to be easy. In fact, when I look at the cold, hard facts, it seems monumental to me. How long will it take for us to rest easy again? I admit that my family and I have been placing far too much emphasis on enjoying the extras of life. We've somehow gotten off track with what's most important. Each of us, I think, has willingly taken the road of comfort and expedience when instead we should have pressed hard to finish the work at hand.*

*Lord, is it too late to undo the mess we've made? I wonder. Will you enable us to forge ahead even though the going will be slow and tedious? Help us not become discouraged when we get weary. Show us the path through and make a way for us even today. Please be my guide and provide me with all the discipline I require to live out my life pleasing to you. Let not greed for material wealth put a wall between us. I commit my coming days to you, faithful Lord. I beg your mercy will surround me and that your grace will shore me up whenever I need fresh encouragement. Amen.*

*Every job is a self-portrait of the person who does it. Autograph your work with excellence.*
—*God's Little Devotional Journal for Women*

# No Easy Escape

*U*nder her breath, Lynda fought for control. She wanted to cry foul to the school board members who were quizzing her on her son Brent's recent placement into the underage juvenile detention center. True enough, Brent, along with two buddies, had broken into a nearby schoolyard and painted graffiti all over the school rock before the rival game. They had inadvertently damaged the fence as they made their late-night escapes. Lynda had been shocked and heartsick. She thought Brent was spending the night at his father's home. Her ex-husband had believed that Brent was with Lynda. Certainly, Brent had played them both. Aside from feeling foolish, Lynda was devastated that her son, once on the honor roll, had taken this senseless course of action. Why, Lynda wondered, did Brent feel he needed to bring such attention to himself all the time now—and at the risk of getting in deep trouble for it?

Lynda, a former high school English instructor, now assistant superintendent, felt both angry and embarrassed. As such a high-profile employee in her school district, Lynda was especially shaken by Brent's deliberate affront to the rules. He was most definitely going to be paying the price for his decision, both monetarily and in community service time. But Lynda felt the attack of silent accusations from every quarter. Wasn't anyone willing to cut her or her son some slack? With all the nonverbal cues Lynda was getting, she wasn't surprised by her own defensive response. Lynda was struggling inside and out. Help me, someone, throw me a lifeline here, she silently pleaded. Instead, Lynda continued to face what felt like a wall of stone-faced, pious men and women who wanted to knock her down to the same level as her son. Oh, it hurts, Lynda thought with despair. How will they ever respect me in the same way again after this episode? How can I expect them to? Self-recrimination flew fast through Lynda's mind. Then she stopped herself short, what's been done here that can't be undone? And what did I always tell my students when they were feeling stymied while writing their term papers? Simple advice really. Don't give up, make the needed changes, and stay at the task until you have it right. Good advice, Lynda, now apply it.

*In Thee O Lord, I have taken refuge;*
*Let me never be ashamed.*
—PSALM 71:1

*Dear Lord, why I am struggling so with this inconsequential issue of my reputation? True enough, I am widely known throughout this area. And, I hope, well enough regarded. But now I feel as though I have disappointed my family, friends, and indeed the entire community. Worst of all, I believe I have disappointed you. Lord, I should not be focusing on the passing comments and trivial opinions of those around me. In time, this event will be forgotten. But my loved one may continue to fight against the battles he's mired himself in. Help me set aside any self-protective thoughts and guide me as I attempt to find practical ways to love my child uncondi-tionally. You know that I fluctuate between anger, resent-ment, and pity for him. May my heart be unconditionally loving and fully committed to restoring peace in his life and ours. Lord, please forgive my shortsightedness. Too often I am only concerned about me! Lord, I am ashamed to admit this to you. I pray that from this day on you will guard my heart and mind against the temptation to fall into the blackness of despair and hopelessness. Sometimes my heart is in such upheaval, I feel dizzy with thoughts of retribution. In these moments, I want this wayward one to pay the full price for his choices. Again, this is grievous to admit openly. But as I confess these shortcomings, I ask that you shower your com-passionate forgiveness upon me—today, tomorrow, and throughout my life. I need your touch of goodness, mercy, and grace to see me through this time of testing. Amen.*

*Real God-given power isn't what you exert over others. That's force. Real God-given power is what you exert over yourself. It's the ability to discipline yourself, to exercise control over not only your behavior but over your thoughts and emotions.*
—RICHARD L. GANZ IN *The Secret of Self-Control*

# 3
## Tough Call

Settling down with a cup of steaming hot tea and lemon, Emma snipped the end of the honey swizzle stick and poured its contents into her tea. Swirling the sweetener around with her spoon, Emma sighed. What to do? Emma had just returned to her childhood home with her three children. Her status as a single parent didn't have many benefits but it did afford her some flexibility. Emma's elderly parents would be moving with them into the burgeoning family home within the coming weeks. Over the past several years, Emma's mother and father had turned that inevitable corner of no longer being able to safely live in their home independently. When Mother and Dad made the offer to move Emma and the children with them back into same house where Emma grew up, it seemed too good to be true. So Emma had sold her own smaller home within days and together they purchased the old homestead. Once Emma's folks sold their current place, they would follow Emma and live together in the more spacious house.

Although tea and lemon calmed Emma's nerves most times, even this tranquil setting didn't begin to temper Emma's rising blood pressure. Hadn't her kids just told her how much they relished living in their new home? Hadn't her dad just last week been demanding to be moved over immediately? Hadn't her mom given her the OK to have a contractor come out and erect a cement wheelchair ramp? Hadn't Emma already moved all of her own belongings as well as many vans full of her parents' goods to their home? To the entire above, yes! So it was understandable that Emma felt as though her world was spinning off its axis after she received the call from her mother with the news they decided not to move to the homestead after all. Shock? Dismay? Emma was uncertain as to how to handle this devastating news flash. Although it was certainly unwanted, Emma admitted to having a small, niggling premonition that her mother just might change her mind at the eleventh hour.

*"Because of the devastation of the afflicted, because of the groaning of the needy,*
*Now I will arise," says the Lord; "I will set him in the safety for which he longs."*
—PSALM 12:5

*Dear Lord, can it be that my parents have switched gears on me again? Even now I'm still mired in disbelief. I've asked myself a dozen times if I correctly heard my mother verbalize her change of heart. Why is this happening? Why now? Can I handle another change? Am I up to this complete turn-around? Again? Oh Lord, I realized going into this situation that it would not be easy. Yet to have sold our home and moved only to do it a second time in a few months' time is just too much to ask. I need you, Lord, more than ever before to come to me and quiet my troubled heart. My mind is literally consumed with disdain for what my parents have done. Please undertake for me now. Enable me by your abundant grace to forgive and let go of this offense.*

*Take me under your wings and give me all that I require to serve my parents and my children. I believe you have called me to offer my strength and support to those I love. Yet I am wavering now, afraid of what the future may hold for me. Undergird me with your resilience and lend me your strong and mighty hands of support. Lord, take this puzzling circumstance and bring good out of it. Change hearts where change is required. Soften the hard edges of personalities and conform us to your son Jesus. Provide wisdom and understanding so that peace might reign supreme. Above all, teach me how to demonstrate your unconditional love and acceptance—unconditionally. Amen.*

*Reach out and take God's hand. Step over the boundary into the unknown and let his tide of love and grace carry you. The life of faith is lived on a need-to-know basis.*
—JUD WILHITE IN *Faith That Goes the Distance*

# 4

# *Massacre*

*T*he day after a fire swept through their home, Kim and her family circled around the perimeter of their property in small steps. When warned that the remaining house structure was still too unstable for them to begin a "search and rescue" for any undamaged valuables, Kim's face betrayed her. Awash in grief, she slowly sidestepped strewn fragments of her house that had crumbled outward as it burned. "Destroyed, it's all gone now," Kim lamented. As she mentally started tabulating all that they would need to replace, Kim felt sick. "Take me back to your house," she told her parents. After making another attempt to emotionally regroup, Kim continued to fight the waves of nausea that would suddenly take her by storm. Where to begin? What to do first? How does one tackle the immense task of rebuilding not only one's home but also everything that lay within it?

Slowly, with her family and friends' assistance, Kim and her family got the insurance claims filed. A cash advance arrived for needed personal items, but they still had to decide whether to rebuild their home or buy another one. Not sure what else to do, Kim and some friends, along with her teens, went to dig around through the heap of debris that used to be their home. They had on heavy work boots and thick gloves, and they had an empty truck to fill—if there was anything worth salvaging. After a couple of hours of work, what they'd been able to salvage didn't amount to much. Blinking back tears, Kim peeked in the truck bed, and something inside her died again. As they all drove back to Kim's parents' home, the friends told her that they needed to make a stop. "Fine," Kim replied numbly, and thought bleakly to herself, I've got no home to return to anyway.

Some twenty minutes later Kim and a crew of family and friends were assembling outside her church. Surprised and taken aback, Kim suspected that this gathering had something to do with her, but she wasn't sure what it could be. "We're here to help get you set up for housekeeping until you move into a permanent place," one friend announced. "We all have a few used, but still nice items we'd like to donate to your family. And once we're finished here, a few of the ladies are going to take you and your kids shopping for clothes and such. And we all pitched in for you to have a new family portrait taken." Kim, aghast, simply stood in shock. Where did all these people come from? All this goodwill? "Just say yes," Kim's friend nudged her. But Kim couldn't say anything, so she just nodded weakly in agreement. A small smile finally reached her heart for the first time in many days.

*The generous man will be prosperous,*
*And he who waters will himself be watered.*
—PROVERBS 11:25

*Dear Lord, today I saw firsthand how miraculously you orchestrated provision for my every need. I was low, so very discouraged. And then you brought together a group of people who expressed their commitment and love toward my family and me in the most loving ways. Not only did they respond with care and sympathy, they have come alongside me and helped steady me as I traverse this painful loss. I could not have been more amazed when they gathered around me to offer goods of their own. Some, I know, sacrificed greatly to give to us. I thank you, Lord, for blessing me with these faithful friends. They are showing me that I am not alone. No matter what I may have to face in the coming months and years; I have a resource greater than any bank account. Though my heart continues to ache because of all we have lost, another part of me is so very grateful for your touch of goodness. I see it all around me. Each day, you truly have bestowed new mercies upon our lives. And my spirit is comforted in the knowledge that you will keep us safe. Nothing can tear us from your faithful grip. Today let my countenance reflect your mercies. Amen.*

*If you laugh a lot, when you are older all your wrinkles will be in the right places.*
—BARBARA JOHNSON IN *Look Who's Laughing!*

# 5

# No Place to Call Home

Liz spent the morning with her lawyer, who had been encouraging her to settle quickly and agree to her estranged husband's divorce terms. Maybe Liz wasn't savvy enough, but after twenty years of marriage, what Kyle was offering didn't seem fair. After all, hadn't Liz worked full-time plus to put her orthodontist husband through school? Didn't she later on pass up career opportunities of her own to raise their two children? Somehow the whole nightmarish scene was threatening to spin even further out of control. The most recent point of contention was who would get the house. If Liz signed the papers as they now read, she would have less than six months to find another place to live. Liz would get a one-time cash settlement, a meager alimony payment for the next seven years, and child support until their oldest turned eighteen.

As her lawyer added up the assets Liz would receive, she continued to fight a sense of mistrust. "I'm not signing anything today," and with that, Liz took the papers and left. As she drove toward her home, Liz realized that there was no way she and the kids could continue living in their spacious house. Even with the monthly alimony payments and her part-time job income, it wouldn't be enough. So Liz struggled with yet another eruption of anger toward her soon-to-be ex-spouse. Feeling her rage surge through her, Liz pulled off to the side of the road to calm down before she arrived home and had to tell her teen sons about the implications of her meeting. Lord, she prayed, I am angrier now than I have ever been. But I want to do what's right for your sake. Will you somehow give me whatever it is I need to refrain from lambasting my husband to our sons? I need to put all my confidence in you now. Lord, please hear me when I pray.

*Trust in the Lord forever,*
*For in God the Lord, we have an everlasting Rock.*
—ISAIAH 26:4

*Dear Lord, I come before you now, like a beggar reaching for a crumb from your table. Oh Lord, I am in a sad state. I am dealing with myriad exhausting challenges. Even as my mind stops to consider what I must do yet this day, I am beyond weary. I feel depleted, deserted, and devastated. What must I do to gain my bearings again? All around me, my life as I knew it is crumbling, shattering at my feet. I am barely able to muster up the strength to complete even the most menial of tasks. Will you come to my aid even now? Boost my reservoir of strength and enable me to meet the challenges of the day with complete confidence in your sustaining strength.*

*And Lord, as I continue to face injustice, at least as I perceive it, will you help me stand firm in my convictions?*

*Help me respond with integrity and truth. Let me not give in to revenge or petty arguments. I pray that you would instill in me a sense of purpose that is far above any desire for personal gain. Let me daily recognize that I am now the leader in my small family. What my children see me doing, saying, and asking for will have an impact on them. They are fighting battles of their own right now, and trust is a big issue. I can see them looking to me for direction and strength; even this can overwhelm me at times. I want to live through this catastrophe with my reputation intact. Please, Lord, lend your grace to me to accomplish this monumental task. When all the dust settles, it will be just you and me, and I want nothing between us—not guilt, remorse, or the sin of bitterness. Set me free, Lord. Place my feet upon a high place beyond the reaches of today's pain. Let my soul rejoice in the sweet communion we can share. Despite the betrayal I have endured, Lord, you will always be my truest friend and guide. I offer my gratitude to you now, and I praise you for who you are. Amen.*

*Lasting leadership is grounded in character. Character produces respect. Respect produces trust. And trust motivates followers.*
—JOHN MACARTHUR IN *Twelve Ordinary Men*

# 6

## *Unfinished Business*

$\mathcal{A}$ manda copied the treatment schedule for the upcoming six weeks onto her daily calendar. It would be rough, she admitted, trying to reorganize and fit everything into what had already been planned while she underwent an additional course of radiation. Oh why didn't I plan better? Amanda lamented. Because you never expected to have your cancer recur, she thought grimly. Amanda stifled back the tears, again. She knew her chances for beating this cancer were narrowing with every recurrence. But she didn't want to give up hope. Amanda had two young children to raise yet, a husband she loved, and a whole life stretching before her. Or did she?

When Amanda was first diagnosed with cancer, she struggled to accept it. After a time, she did reconcile herself to the hard truth that she was in the fight of her life. Amanda underwent radiation, then surgery. A year later, more radiation and then more surgery. And now, another course of radiation. Amanda tried to brace herself for what lay beyond the next few weeks. But she didn't feel brave enough to face death square. She needed more time, time to cope and adjust, time to live. But with no alternative open to her, Amanda realized she had to focus on today's needs alone. She simply could not summon up the resolve to look beyond the present daily demands, and this lack of resolve was draining her of precious life energy. *I need to set this aside,* Amanda told herself, *and I need to quiet my heart and soul. Refocus on the positive and allow you, Lord, to bring me to a safe place, a place of peace.*

*My soul waits in silence for God only;*
*From Him is my salvation.*
—Psalm 62:1

*Dear Lord, I recall a time not so very long ago when death and dying were vague, nondescript topics of conversation. Never did it occur to me that I may well find myself becoming one of the statistics. Me, the person who has hardly ever seen a sick day until this disease was discovered. I rarely considered how those with ongoing bouts of illness faced life day after day with courage. Now, I'm in awe of their ability to face their futures with hope and optimism. I'm not made of such stern stuff. Rather, I want comfort, security, and promises of a pain-free existence. Lord, I am so frail it scares me sometimes. I put on the brave face for my loved ones, but inside I'm trembling so. The very thought of another course of uncomfortable treatments, and with no guarantee of success, summons up the very worst of my fears. Why should I go through that agony again if not to be cured?*

*And then my mind is continually playing out the worst-case scenarios for my family. If I die, how will they cope in my absence? My children are so young, will they remember me? Lord, calm my upset heart. I beg you draw near to me now and wrap your loving arms around me. Encompass me in your security and strength. I am in such dire need for your loving touch upon my heart and mind, I cannot draw another breath without you. Please Lord, show me the way through this hideousness. I am undone. Nothing I can say, do, or think makes a whit of difference to my situation. It is truly beyond my control. I come before you now, pleading for a miracle. I know that my life literally hangs in the balance between this life and the next. And I ask you for the courage I require to live out every day allotted to me with good grace and good humor. Help me turn the tables on this dreaded condition and offer life-giving hope to all I meet. Let not this disease master me. Enable me to live with faith, vision, and purpose throughout each and every day you bless me with. I hold out my hands to you now, Lord, in anticipation of your gentle assurance. Amen.*

> *The goal of silent or contemplative prayer is to bring your mind, emotions, and spirit to complete stillness, to experience a profound state of rest. This deep, inner rest is wonderful, spreading through your entire being.*
> —DAVID HAZARD IN *Reducing Stress*

# 7

# Empty Nest

When Brenda walked in the door to her small two-bedroom home, the first sound she heard was a strident voice yelling demeaning retorts from somewhere near the kitchen. Striding forward to quell the argument before it turned into a full-blown fight, Brenda was immediately taken aback by what she saw. Her entire kitchen looked as though it had been ransacked. Flour was strewn all over the counter, sugar spilled on the floor, broken eggs lay in and around the sink. And there stood her two sons right in the middle of the mess. When they stopped their feuding long enough to notice Brenda standing there, arms akimbo and glaring, they had the good grace to look a tad sheepish. "What is going on here?" Brenda demanded. The two boys' voices were raised in a rush to present their own side, growing louder and more insistent until Brenda couldn't decipher either one. "Quiet!" she boomed. "Get this mess cleaned up now and then we'll talk."

Exiting the kitchen before she gave in to her own rising anger, Brenda took off her coat, laid down her purse and briefcase, and marched into her own room. After changing clothes, Brenda decided that she needed some more time to cool off before addressing her sons. She lay down on the bed and could faintly hear a broom being swept across the floor and the garbage disposal running. Good, she thought, at least the room will be cleaned up before I have to go in and start making dinner. As Brenda quieted herself, she couldn't stop that rush of regret that so frequently accompanied these minor skirmishes between her kids. She had to admit it: at times like these she really missed her ex-husband. But he wasn't around anymore, and Brenda was smart enough to realize that all in all, even her feeble attempts to make up for his absence was healthier for the boys than his disturbing presence. Still, Brenda found herself longing for someone else to shoulder some of the parenting responsibility. And she realized, I'm lonely too. God, she prayed, I'm back at square one today, still wishing I had someone to lean on—even though I know better. Help me, please, to learn that you're always waiting for me to call on you for what I need most.

*Let us therefore draw near with confidence to the throne of grace, that we may receive mercy and may find grace to help in time of need.*
—HEBREWS 4:16

*Dear Lord, I'm back with more petitions for help. I'm running on empty again—seemingly because I can't get it through my head that I need to bask in your presence each and every day. For some odd reason, I allow myself to become so distracted by life's demands that I neglect my relationship with you. I sometimes wonder if I'll ever get it right. How many more desolate seasons will I traverse before I finally come to my senses? Lord, I am sorry for my poor choices. Too often, too late, I suddenly wake up and realize I've been putting my heart's energy into the wrong places. I am not a wise investor, this is sorely apparent. Will you help me break this destructive pattern I've set up for myself? I no longer want to be a wanderer. I need to be planted, and firmly so, at your feet. Lord, as your child, I know you love me. I also realize you are always close beside me. Yet you understand that I long for human companionship as well. I pray that you will help me live contentedly in my present state of singleness. Help me relax and appreciate the blessings of this stage of my life. And there are many reasons for rejoicing. I would ask that you continue to guide my steps as a parent, enabling me to be both loving and firm with my children. Make up for my lack, Lord! I count upon you for the strength to even finish out this day. As I have many times before, I lay down my burdens at your feet. And I ask for the wisdom to leave them there. Amen.*

*We spend so much time chasing after the baubles of the world, we're bankrupt when it comes to the treasures of the holy. We want joy and beauty, but we want them without having to stay connected to the One who gives them.*
—PHILIP GULLEY IN *Front Porch Tales*

# 8

## Ransomed Resources

$\mathcal{M}$eg hung up the telephone in disbelief. It couldn't be true, she lamented. Joe's life insurance money gone, every penny lost. Didn't I do as Joe had suggested before he died? I went to our friend and invested it just as Joe told me to. I listened and trusted my entire savings to someone who promised that my money would be safe. Goodness knows I'm not a gambler, so how could this have happened? Joe and I agreed many times over the years to allow our funds to grow slowly—safely. I cannot fathom how this ever occurred. There must be some mistake. Surely, my investor, our friend, can make this up to me.

And just where does this turn of events place me now? I was planning on retiring in the spring. Now that won't be possible. I'll need every extra cent due me from a full retirement package. Ever since Joe died it's been rough enough. But I've always had my hopes set on finishing up this final year of teaching and then traveling to spend more time with my grandchildren. At last, I felt I could be of help to my own grown kids and ease their burdens. Instead, I may become a weight upon them. Lord, let it not be! Give me the grace I need at this moment to make sense of this untimely loss. I ask you for your wisdom to guide me and show me how to proceed despite this tremendous setback.

In you alone I must trust, but everything in me is screaming for restitution. I want my money back! Lord, will you please direct me even now? Help me settle down and pursue a course that is both wise and prudent. Help me connect with someone who knows more about these financial ins and outs than I do. Above all, put a seal of your peace around my heart.

*The Lord also will be a stronghold for the oppressed,*
*A stronghold in times of trouble,*
*And those who know Thy name will put their trust in Thee;*
*For Thou, O Lord, hast not forsaken those who seek Thee.*
—PSALM 9:9–10

*Dear Lord, it is a wonder to me that in all my years I've never fretted about money before. I've never been wealthy, yet I have always been so certain you would provide for my needs. Perhaps it's because I'm on my own now that this unexpected setback has sent me reeling. I admit to feeling overwhelmed and frightened. How I wish I could turn back the clock and undo this tragic error. Yet another part of me would not wish it so because I know that you will accomplish your good work within my heart even through, and maybe because of, this circumstance. My heart is confident that you will see me through this time of financial hardship.*

*I beg you now for a heavenly perspective of this situation. Would you fill my heart and mind with thoughts that calm my restive spirit? Reawaken in me a boldness that declares your faithfulness despite the circumstances. Enlarge my faith and allow me to proclaim your goodness to all I come into contact with. Let me not surrender the joy and peace you've promised to supply me. Give me the strength to endure what I must in order to see this trial to its completion. Mark me for yourself and allow me the privilege of serving you in mighty ways throughout the rest of my life. I am continually reminded of your many promises that entreat us to hunger after you and the treasure of your love over and above all other pursuits. I pray that you will nurture in my soul a driving passion to know you better through this time of struggle. I do delight in you, and your ways are indeed righteous and holy. Amen.*

*Suffering carries with it a type of forced dependence, which casts our lives before the power and presence of God. It takes away our doomed efforts to save ourselves so that we can be rescued by the One who knows exactly how to save us.*
—JAMES EMERY WHITE IN *Life-Defining Moments*

# 9
## Shake Down

During her lunch break, Chelsea ate her salad and sipped her coffee. Then, as was her routine, she spent the next fifteen minutes or so sorting through some mail she hadn't had time to read the evening before. Although she tossed most of the envelopes after a quick glance, a few letters caught her eye. Chelsea opened the lightly tinted gray envelope, the kind her employer used. A letter, hmmm. Chelsea wondered what could be important enough to warrant a letter in between pay periods. Scanning the contents, Chelsea felt her heart plummet. Not this year, she wanted to cry. We're barely meeting our bills as it is. Chelsea couldn't think straight. What, being laid off indefinitely? Certainly she had heard the rumors that a small portion of the company might be temporarily forced to go on unemployment, but with her seniority she had not worried about being among these unfortunates. Still, there it was, plain as day and in black and white. Chelsea, like the rest of her group, would work their regular schedules through the month's end, then she would apply for unemployment. For how long? Chelsea wondered. But the letter didn't elaborate. I need to talk with my supervisor this afternoon, she decided.

Trying not to panic, Chelsea could only think about her once fully employed husband, now a full-time college student, who worked just ten to fifteen hours a week at the college library. With his meager paycheck and her unemployment benefits, Chelsea doubted they could meet their monthly financial obligations. She wanted to rush in and demand an audience with whoever had made this disastrous decision. But she didn't. *I'm not alone in this*, Chelsea concluded. *There are at least a hundred men and women facing exactly the same hardships I am. And sadly, many of them have never called upon you, Lord, to rescue them.*

---

*The Lord shall reign forever and ever.*
—EXODUS 15:18

*Dear Lord, even now, so many seasons since I first put my heart and soul into your hands, I continue to linger in mistrust. I find myself in a downward spiral of my own making. Instead of facing a difficult situation squarely with the shield of faith, I fall into despair and am tempted to give up before the battle begins. Lord, please forgive my lack of courage. How is it that I am so weak? Have I not witnessed your hand of protection time and again? I wonder when I will learn to rest easy in your provision for me. Perhaps I do not know you well enough yet? You, who are unchanging, continue to reach down with care and concern to lift me back up and set me aright. Still, I fail to comprehend your sovereignty. I would rather wallow in my own despair than put the needed effort into standing strong with the faith you've allotted me.*

*Forgive me, Lord, and begin a new work within me now. Even as I am forced to enter a time of cutbacks, I must do so with good grace. Help me see past my own discomforts and uncertainties so that I may offer some measure of encouragement to those in my circumstances. Somehow, let my life become a beacon of hope to others who may be floundering as well. I pray that none of this pain is wasted. Let the good fruits of wisdom and understanding flourish even now. Turn my eyes upon you, Lord, for all that I need in the coming weeks and months. Teach me your ways, and let not any adversity tear me from your presence. Hold me, in your faithful grip, today, tomorrow, and always. Let me awaken in the morning with my first thought being of you. Compel me, Lord, to make my utmost priority that of learning more about who you are. For the sake of your son, Jesus, these things I pray. Amen.*

*To pray is to change. Prayer is the central avenue God uses to transform us. . . . The closer we come to the heartbeat of God the more we see our need and the more we desire to be conformed to Christ.*
—RICHARD J. FOSTER IN *Celebration of Discipline*

# 10
# Twilight

Under the circumstances, Taylor begged off from the yearly spa weekend she and her three best friends had planned. For over ten years, Taylor and her girlfriends from college had met in a midway locale to while away the hours getting pampered by the best. In between treatment sessions, Taylor and friends would gleefully plan where to shop, eat, and what type of evening entertainment to enjoy. The time always went by fast, but for Taylor, who only saw these ladies every twelve months, it was time and money well invested. So with great reluctance, Taylor declined this particular winter's get together. She wondered if any excuse would be good enough for her pals. Taylor knew that they relished the getaway weekend as much as she did, and each of them guarded that time protectively.

But Taylor also knew that she couldn't leave home just now, not with her son Zach's troubles. What had it been, six weeks of rehab already? When would he be coming home? Taylor mused. Maybe as soon as next week, if he meets all his obligations for the next seven days. Excited yet pensive, Taylor considered how Zach's homecoming would affect the rest of the family. Sadly, Taylor admitted how peaceful it had been with Zach away. As much as Taylor loved her son, she literally despised the addictions he carried with him. Drugs and alcohol abuse had given her and the family no end of sleepless nights and pain-ridden days when they had no idea if or when Zach would ever come home again. Certainly, this treatment center appeared to have helped Zach; Taylor prayed it was so, but she couldn't help but be wary of any "supposed" changes in his behavior. Hadn't he fooled them before? Indeed. Well, Taylor said to herself, even though I can't steal away for the weekend and gain some moral support, I can ask that my closest friends remember me and the family in their own prayers.

*It was for freedom that Christ set us free; therefore keep standing firm and do not be subject again to a yoke of slavery.*
—GALATIANS 5:1

*Dear Lord, today I was momentarily reminded again of how this dreaded addiction, this compulsion, has taken our entire family captive. Lord, I wish it were not so. Yet all that I have said and done has not changed the truth of the matter. My loved one is so tightly chained to misery—much of it due to his own poor choices. Yet I love him so. I ache for him to be free from this burden. And a part of me is skeptical as well. How many times have I heard the pleas for another chance? How many sleepless nights did I lie awake waiting for the telephone to ring? For reconciliation that never happened? Lord, I am at the end of what I know what to do. I can no longer continue in the same vein as before. I am hopeful, to a point, that perhaps this will be the fork in the road for our family. I understand that I must never give up on this loved one. But how do I keep my sanity and watch him suffer so? And is it possible to protect the rest of the family from this danger? I do not suppose to have all the answers. Surely, you have watched me muddle through these many years. But I, too, have come to a crossroads of sorts. I will not allow the sins of one to drag down and destroy the rest of us. I realize that many would not understand this decision. It does sound harsh even to my ears. Yet I know it to be the path I must now follow. Give me the strength to do what is best, what is healthiest for all of us. Let me not hesitate to invite discipline to bear upon any future offences. Give me what I require to see long term, Lord. For I know that quick fixes might appease for the moment, but they do nothing for the heart and soul. Day by day, be our closest companion and guide. Amen.*

*He leads me. God isn't behind me, yelling, "Go!" He is ahead of me, bidding, "Come!" He is in front, clearing the path, cutting the brush, showing the way. . . . He leads us. He tells us what we need to know when we need to know it.*
—MAX LUCADO IN *Traveling Light for Mothers*

# II
## Visitation Rights

$\mathcal{K}$ ate left her lunch sitting in the front seat of her truck, along with her heart. Given her tumultuous emotions at the time, Kate didn't think it wise to chance eating before this weekly group session. As in times past, Kate knew the routine. She would be carefully checked before being admitted into the hospital and once inside, closely monitored during the entire visit. Todd, her alcoholic husband, had now gone without a drink for twenty-one days. Once his body detoxed from the alcohol poisoning, he was pushed into therapy almost immediately. Todd, who had been through this routine before, was far more comfortable in this sterile, controlled environment. Kate suspected it was because Todd didn't have to make any decisions for himself. Everything from what he consumed and wore to what he participated in throughout the highly regimented program was already decided for him. Still, Kate understood that in order for Todd to get better, he needed to work through the system step by step.

Unlike Todd, Kate detested the place. She couldn't wait to get the next hour over and done with so she could escape back into the real world. But she was committed to Todd's overcoming his problems, so week after week, Kate determined to willingly be part of her husband's recovery program. At least, she concurred, I get to see and meet all the people Todd's been spending so much time with now. Later on, I'll have a clearer idea of who and what he's referring to. Maybe that in itself will give me a better perspective of his progress, too. Trying to come up with additional reasons for laying bare her own soul and watching her wounded spouse do the same in the midst of fifteen to twenty other adults, Kate quickly offered up a silent prayer for the strength to do what needed done.

*And whoever exalts himself shall be humbled; and whoever humbles himself shall be exalted.*
—MATTHEW 23:12

*Dear Lord, thank for you enabling me to see this period of setbacks—my time, my marriage—through an eternal perspective. You alone know how I fight against such trespasses. I am frequently frustrated when expected to pitch in and give more than my fair share. I understand that this attitude is both selfish and sinful. At a time when my loved one is so very needy, I am bucking against giving all I can to aid him. What is wrong with me? I sometimes suspect that I am more troubled inwardly than my loved one; I simply do not manifest the symptoms. Will you supply me with all I need to be of support?*

*And Lord, please help me continue to look to you for my strength and solace. It is true, I want nothing more than life the way it used to be. Uncomplicated and simple. Yet somehow, that notion of reality was never quite accurate, was it? Always brimming right below the surface was a whole sea of unresolved issues and pain. Even now, I tremble when I think about what we've had to endure. And today, when I must face yet another difficult and uncomfortable task, I pray that you will be with me. Clothe me with a humble heart, Lord. Show me how to speak with kindness and truth. Let not my instinct for self-preservation take over so that I am unable or unwilling to do good. I pray that I will be both wise and insightful. Help me anticipate potential pitfalls and give me the sense to avoid them. I also ask that you continue to bring genuine healing to my loved one. He struggles so desperately that often we live in a hopeless relationship. Give us whatever it is that we require to make lasting changes in our lives. Encircle us with your protection and provision. Make your presence known to us throughout the coming days and weeks. I pray that our lives might be transformed even now. Lord, we are at your mercy, as always, we depend upon your grace to meet us here. Amen.*

*After giving, giving, giving so many things, He warns us about forgetting Him. How easy, when blessed, to adopt a presumptuous, arrogant spirit. Indulgence begins as erosion within that leads to indifference, which ultimately results in independence.*
—CHARLES R. SWINDOLL IN *Making the Weak Family Strong*

# 12

# *War Casualties*

t was touch and go for a while as Rose attempted to remain calm and not give in to her rising anger. But she took a deep breath, again, and took her time purposefully explaining how it might have been more prudent to follow up on the latest lead rather than shout expletives into the phone. Rose tried to make her wayward daughter and son-in-law understand that she hired this particular private detective to help them find their daughter, her only grand-daughter. Rose patiently explained that from now on, she would be the contact person, not either of them. Surprisingly, the couple sitting before her didn't argue the point. Undoubtedly, they had more important things to do than concern themselves with their runaway daughter, Reann. Still, Rose was grateful. Now she was free to do all she could to locate her granddaughter and attempt to bring her home to her own house this time. Maybe, Rose thought hopefully, Reann will stay put and finish her education. That is, if we ever find her again.

Gathering her coat, purse, and keys, Rose said her good-byes and drove home. As soon as she walked in the door, she checked her answering machine. Nothing. Well, what did I expect? Rose chided herself for being so unrealistic. I just spoke to the detective this morning; certainly he wouldn't have any more news for me this soon. Still, I have to continue to hope, don't I? So Rose busied herself around her home. She did some light cleaning, a load of wash, and started to prepare dinner. Whenever she worked around the kitchen, Rose couldn't stop the stream of memories of when she and Reann used to happily buzz around making cookies, cinnamon rolls, and sugar cake. So long ago, Rose reminisced. How was it that my darling granddaughter suddenly transformed into a young woman I hardly recognize? Certainly, her parents were at fault, leaving her alone so much and not putting her needs above their own. Oh, how awful it was to watch them destroy their family bit by bit, Rose thought back. And now it's been five weeks since we've last heard from Reann. God only knows where she is now, Rose thought despairingly. "Indeed, only God does know and who better than to watch over her," Rose declared suddenly.

*The fear of the Lord is the beginning of knowledge;*
*Fools despise wisdom and instruction.*
—PROVERBS 1:7

*Dear Lord, I am unsure how to bring my petition in prayer this day. I fully understand what my heart's inclination is to ask for. I want my family restored and wholly healed. But I cannot demand such things from you. Not now, not ever. You are a holy God, set apart from the race of man. The divide is so great, no one can fully understand your greatness. Yet I long for intimacy with you, Lord. I am in dire need of your refreshing touch. Will you reach down and meet me here? Even now, I'm parched for lack of your spirit. I've tried to mend all this pain in my own small ways. But nothing I do seems to make any lasting difference. I now see that it is only by your work of redemption in both my heart and in the hearts of those I love that any permanent healing will come to pass. Please do not abandon us in our present state. Come quickly to us, I beg. At this moment, my thoughts are confused and my strength is slack. Each day brings new disappointment and despair claws at my heart's door. Protect me from unseen enemies that threaten me during my darkest hours. Take not your presence away from me, Lord. I count upon you every minute. And I ask that you continue to protect my loved one from harm. Though we do not know the where, or even the why, you see all. Please, Lord, extend your hand even to the farthest reaches of our world and draw this lost soul back to you. I commit my family into your care and keeping, trusting you to minister your perfect love in every heart. Amen.*

> *I was drought-crisped, and now I'm rain-reliant. Accepting what comes, then offering it back. Letting go of control. Learning this thing called prayer.*
> —CINDY CROSBY IN *By Willoway Brook*

# PART TWO

## Relational Setbacks

Friendships go sour, marriages take a downturn, mother-daughter relationships are strained, work associates gossip unfairly—is there any quarter where solid, loving, and trusting women can thrive emotionally and spiritually? Assuredly so. Yet within the confines of every relationship there exist two desperately flawed elements, you and me. The hard truth is that all relationships take the utmost care and maintenance to keep them healthy. Whether we decide to invest in these precious commodities we call friends and family is our choice alone. But it is a richer world for every step we take toward another person.

# 13
# Sudden Good-Byes

Well, it was done. After fourteen grueling weeks on the market, Melanie finally sold her house. With great relief, Melanie made a big show of flourishing her pen and signing on the numerous lines of the contract handed her by the realtor. They all laughed. Melanie had been looking to sell her two-bedroom home so she could move into a condo for some time. Two years at least, if her recollections were accurate. It was right after she transferred to another department and took on a new position at her computer software firm that Melanie decided with all the traveling she'd be doing, a house wasn't so important to her any longer.

Once that Melanie was gone for five or six days at a time, the last thing she looked forward to was coming home to mow the grass and do yard work on her days off. Simplify, Melanie told herself. And she couldn't have been more pleased with her new low-maintenance condo. At last I can enjoy the little time I'm in town to see friends and keep up with what's going on in their lives. Friends, the thought made Melanie's heart lurch. One friend in particular caused Melanie no end of heartache. I might have taken the right steps in ensure a more uncomplicated life in the home ownership department, but I certainly still have to deal with the bitter vestiges of one friendship gone sour.

Saying her good-byes and her thanks to her realtor, Melanie got into her car and started toward home. What should have been a day for celebrating had inadvertently turned into another afternoon of regrets. How had the breach occurred, Melanie asked herself for the hundredth time? Jackie and I have been friends for years, what exactly went wrong? Melanie never had understood why her once dear friend had suddenly stopped calling and coming over. Even after I pointedly questioned Jackie, she never did come clean, pondered Melanie. I still don't even know if it was something I did or perhaps didn't do. Lord, help me find a way to make contact again with my friend. Give me an opening that might help us clear the air and start over. Maybe a condo warming party would be in order?

*And God is able to make all grace abound to you, that always having all sufficiency in everything, you may have an abundance for every good deed.*
—2 CORINTHIANS 9:8

*Dear Lord, I come before you today full of regret and perhaps even some shame. I am totally mystified as to why my friend has cut off our friendship. I do not understand her actions. I have tried, Lord; you know how many times I have attempted to make this painful situation right. But nothing I have done has worked. I am still no closer to the truth than before.*

*Will you give me a renewed desire to extend my hand of friendship again to this person? Lord, I admit to not wanting to be rejected again. It stings and the hurt runs deep. Still, I am convinced that I should make another attempt at reconciliation. Perhaps now that some time has passed, my friend will be able and willing to talk. Help me to know the best way to approach her, Lord. Give me a sensitive spirit, a forgiving one. Maybe I have offended her without realizing it, if so, enable me to humbly ask for her pardon. And let not pride or anger on my part drive a further wedge between us.*

*I do miss our friendship. Often I am reminded of the good times we had together as well as how we supported one another through the tough stretches. If there is any way that we might rebuild our relationship, I pray that you will begin your good work within both our hearts today. Help me extend a gracious hand of compassion and understanding to my former friend. Let peace abound between us. I commit this situation into your capable hands once more. Amen.*

*The notion that our lives are like the eternal cycle of the seasons does not deny the struggle or the joy, the loss or the gain, the darkness or the light, but encourages us to embrace it all—and to find in all of it opportunities for growth.*
—PARKER J. PALMER IN *Let Your Life Speak*

# 14

## Deferred Desires

ighteen-year-old Kelsey sat on her porch swing mind-
lessly absorbing the snatches of conversation drifting in
from the adjacent kitchen window. She heard a tense voice
raise a notch in both volume and intensity. Kelsey drew in
another quick breath and held it. Waiting. She was listening
in earnest now. Oh, Lord, Kelsey prayed, please let your
peace reign in our home. Pausing with bated breath, Kelsey
felt her knuckles burn as she gripped the metal link chain
that held the swing in place. Let it go, she told herself.
Don't enter into the fray again. Just pray. Almost unwittingly, Kelsey dropped her hands to her side and gave up the
fight.

It didn't seem to matter what she did anyway. Her
parents had argued like this for as long as she could remember. Still, Kelsey never could adjust to their bitter recrimi-
nations. She had tried to play peacemaker more times than
she could count. Ironically, any attempts at smoothing the
troubled waters only seemed to fire the fuel of accusation
between her mom and dad. What puzzled Kelsey most was
how her folks could turn on a dime. One minute they'd be
conversing with an almost casual grace. The next, it was a
battle of the most bitter sort. Kelsey had cried many tears at
night and into the early morning hours after being awakened

by angry shouts and slamming doors. Next fall, three short months from now, Kelsey would be leaving home for college. In a way, she was glad to escape all the conflict surrounding her home life. Still, she agonized over her parents' crumbling relationship. She sometimes wondered whether her dad would even be living at home when she returned for the holidays.

So, in these last months before leaving for good, Kelsey wondered exactly what her responsibility was toward her parents. Aside from praying for them, what else should she do? It was a question that haunted her daily. Kelsey had once confided in an older woman from their church. What was it this woman had encouraged Kelsey to do? Something about making sure Kelsey took time to pray for her parents and then closing the door to the problem for the rest of the day. Kelsey puzzled over this suggestion. Finally, she understood. Her elderly friend wanted Kelsey to trust God to handle a situation out of her control and to keep on living her life despite the poor choices her parents continued to make.

*Hope deferred makes the heart sick,*
*But desire fulfilled is a tree of life.*
—PROVERBS 13:12

*Dear Lord, I'm unsure of how to handle the conflict in my home. I want to play peacemaker and get in between the combatants and tell them to back off and head to their own corners to cool down. I feel like I should be doing something, anything, to make our home a peaceful place. But it doesn't seem to matter what I attempt to do, they still continue to wage a battle beyond my comprehension. Lord, I pray that you will quiet the waters of contention within my family. Help each one of us turn to you for our comfort and strength when tempted to react in anger or bitterness. Let your good and abundant grace flow through each of us. Fill us with your Holy Spirit and let self-control be evident in every con-versation into which we enter. At times, I confess to feeling wracked with guilt and hopelessness. I wonder if it's my fault that my family is so full of strife. I pray that you will give me what I require to live in a manner that brings glory and honor to you. And let me not give in to the despair that comes so often. Supply me with the stamina to continue pray-ing for those I love and interceding for their souls. As I come to your throne of grace each day, let me be reminded of your sufficiency and sovereignty. I am so grateful that you indeed do rule and reign over our world. Please take the place of lordship over me and let my family see their need to do the same. Amen.*

> *But the nearness of Christ is often granted first to those whose need mandates that presence. Jesus draws near to the needy pre-cisely because the self-sufficient seem to have all the company they crave.*
> —CALVIN MILLER IN *Jesus Loves Me*

# 15
# *Blissful Beginnings?*

Kathryn toyed with the engagement and wedding rings she had just picked up from the jeweler. "Everything's intact, no loose gems, and the settings are securely in place," the jeweler assured Kathryn. "You should have no trouble with them." Thanks a bunch, Kathryn had wanted to retort. Inwardly, she was hoping there had been something wrong with the rings so she could have left them at the jeweler's for a while. That would have been reason enough not to wear them, Kathryn thought sadly. Unlike her diamonds, Kathryn's marriage was not properly "set." Fumbling for her keys, Kathryn pulled them out of her purse and inserted the car key into the ignition; the engine turned over. As the car sputtered to life Kathryn stifled groan of resentment against her husband of six months. It's amazing that Steve feels it necessary to drive our one reliable vehicle, my car in fact, while I get burdened with his old clunker. Kathryn checked her rearview mirror and began backing out until a honk from somewhere in her blind spot alerted her to stop. She looked again and still didn't see anyone in the way; cautiously backing out a bit further, Kathryn spied the miniscule sports car in question. It, too, made her angry. Here I am driving this old boat, I can't see a thing, and I'll be lucky if I make it home at all.

And there's that guy driving a car that probably cost more than our entire assets combined. It isn't fair, Kathryn complained. Pitying her unenviable circumstances, Kathryn drove home, her anger propelling her further with every mile she traveled.

How exactly has this happened? Kathryn asked herself for the umpteenth time. Just where did our relationship go wrong? Did we ever love each other? Or were we just so eager to get married that we neglected to face the truth that we are two very different people heading in two different directions? With nowhere else to turn, Kathryn decided to offer up a half-hearted prayer, but as she did she wondered if God would even hear. Still, Kathryn thought, I've got nothing else to lose by trying.

*But seeing the wind, he became afraid, and beginning to sink, he cried out, saying, "Lord, save me!" And immediately Jesus stretched out His hand and took hold of him, and said to him, "O you of little faith, why did you doubt?"*
—MATTHEW 14:30–31

*Dear Lord, I am like one of your disciples, sinking under the circumstances of my own making. I have been afraid. As soon as the winds of adversity blew my way, I gave up in defeat. I am no longer looking to you for deliverance. Instead, I have turned aside and made it clear that I desire no help. My heart has been hard, my spirit cold. Even my once tender emotion is dried up and brittle. Lord, I understand that*

*I am in a difficult position. I also know that I am partly to blame. But at this moment, I am also aware that I am not willing to make any changes. Please help me forsake my anger and bitterness. Make it clear to me that the path I now am on is one of destruction. Lord, in my mind, I realize that I must forgive and learn how to rebuild this relationship. But I am so wearied from past defeats in trying to do so. Will you give me the heart to begin again? I sorely need your touch of gracious strength to ask for a pardon and receive one in return. I am grieved that in so short a time my loved one and I have become so estranged. We are like strangers, perhaps enemies. Every act, every attitude, is attributed to selfishness or self-centeredness. Lord, give us both merciful hearts and enable us to love unconditionally. I admit that my own commitment has wavered and my love has waned in these recent days. I also realize that you alone can bring renewal and restoration. In all honesty, I have little hope, Lord. Will you make up for our lack with your perfect love? I must trust in your strength once again. Amen.*

*We don't tell ourselves we are better; we simply give in to the feeling of satisfaction that we don't share another's weakness. Thus we give in to pride's seductive embrace, slowly at first, but then with increasing abandon, until its hold on our lives becomes obvious to everyone but ourselves.*
—JAMES EMERY WHITE IN *Long Night's Journey into Day*

# 16
## Rocked and Rattled

Sorting through an old box overflowing with family photos, Pam smiled as she gazed at one picture after another. Happier times, no doubt about it, Pam reflected. She placed each tender memory into one of three piles: one for putting into her scrapbooks, another for pitching, and a third to be tucked away for the time being. As Pam continued rifling through the photos, she realized she was unconsciously separating the keepsakes according to who was depicted in each one. Biting her lip, Pam picked up the pile to be tucked away and noticed that her estranged husband was in every photo. Unwittingly, Pam had placed him and the pain he had wrought on their family as far away mentally as she could. Feeling a twinge of guilty remorse, Pam made a second run through the pictures in question. She debated, just as she had only a few nights before, should I let him move back home or not? Back and forth, Pam tried to come to a decision—one she wouldn't regret this time. But it wasn't that simple. Didn't she have to consider the kids? What would they say if Dad sashayed back into their lives just as casually as he had left? I just don't know, Pam thought concernedly. A part of me never wants to see him again, another part is still holding out hope that things might be better.

What to do? Pam laughed at the irony of it all as she held the photos in her hands. *I can't even decide what to do with a bunch of pictures, let alone decide if I'm ready to rebuild a marriage with a man who left me for no good reason other than he wanted some space. Oh Lord, if I ever needed an extra measure of decision-making know-how, it's now.*

*Make your ear attentive to wisdom,*
*Incline your heart to understanding;*
*For if you cry for discernment,*
*Lift your voice for understanding;*
*If you seek her as silver,*
*And search for her as for hidden treasures;*
*Then you will discern the fear of the Lord,*
*And discover the knowledge of God.*
—PROVERBS 2:2–5

*Dear Lord, I'm in a quandary and not sure how to proceed. Should I or shouldn't I? These contrary thoughts keep humming around in my brain. Am I being stubborn, resistant, unwilling to forgive? Perhaps. Still, the one person who committed to stick with me for the duration has violated that commitment. Lord, how does one learn to forgive such an offence? I'm not sure I even want to pardon this person. I admit it. I want him to suffer as I did, as my children are still suffering. I understand this is not right. I know, deep down, that I can never be free if I refuse to forgive. Yet I am fighting against this principle with every ounce of my being. And the thought of welcoming this person back into my life is almost too much to bear. Can I? Should I? All these unanswered questions loom large in my mind.*

*It's not that I am totally unwilling to start over. I believe I could do so, if I had a guarantee that this person has sincerely changed. That he will never hurt me again. But life offers no such pain-free policies. I am forced to make a decision that may well land me in even more agony than before. Lord, please, give me the wisdom I require to make this important choice. Show me your way. Lead me and guide me with your rod of protection. Undertake for me even now; calm my troubled heart. Bring a generous measure of peace into my life and let the joy of your salvation envelop me completely. Above all, let me not return evil for evil. Rather, let my words be immersed in truth and let integrity guard me. Again, I pray that you will make your will known to me. Let your precepts and principles speak clearly to me as I wash myself anew each day in your good word. Amen.*

*The hardest thing is that it's not just saying a one-time yes. It's waking up every morning and saying yes to God in the midst of the daily pain.*
—Sheila Walsh in *Living Fearlessly*

# 17
## Mindful Words

Diana replayed the message left on their answering machine. Once, twice, three times. Just to be sure she had it right, Diana listened again. No doubt about it, Diana and her husband were being summoned to a special emergency meeting with several of their church's leaders. And she knew why. Jeff, Diana's pastor-husband, had recently put in his resignation effective at the start of the New Year. She understood why Jeff had decided to terminate his pastoral position, but Diana wasn't so certain that others in their congregation would. Jeff had never really wanted to head up a church, the job sort of fell to him when the previous pastor left for another post. Although Jeff had thrived as an associate pastor, when his responsibilities were mainly overseeing the Christian education departments and teaching an adult Sunday School class twice weekly, Jeff didn't want the senior pastor's job. Diana agreed with her husband. Jeff wasn't suited to head up an entire church body. How had he described himself? Organizationally challenged? Or was it administratively deficient? Regardless, Jeff was already lining up a full-time teaching position at the local college. He was thrilled and eager to dig into this new venture. Diana was relieved that they would soon be free of the burdensome weight that Jeff had so struggled under for the past two years.

Yet Diana also felt conflicted. Just how much pressure would be exerted on her and her husband to stay put? It was clear from previous comments that some in other leadership capacities felt Jeff was forsaking the church and his calling as a minister. Diana chafed under those remarks. Still, Diana knew she had to attend the so-called "update meeting" to which they had been beckoned. She knew full well that they were likely to be misunderstood, maybe even maligned, yet it was something they had to do.

*For as the earth brings forth its sprouts,*
*And as a garden causes the things sown in it to spring up,*
*So the Lord God will cause righteousness and praise*
*To spring up before all the nations.*
—ISAIAH 61:11

*Dear Lord, why am I so concerned about the opinions of others? It is disconcerting to me that I care this much. I have tried to put the comments of those who do not understand on the backburner of my mind. I don't want to dwell on such negative thoughts. Yet these tactless remarks linger long after the fact. Lord, I need your strength to overcome this struggle. I am continually tempted to listen to the voice of others over and above your voice. Please forgive me. I admit to fretting and worrying over what someone may think or say about me.*

*I feel so misunderstood, and this recent event has caused my stress level to rise higher yet. As I work through this troubling issue, will you stand beside me and continue to remind me of the truth? I have not been placed here to concern myself with the meddling words of others. I am your child and you have a specific design and purpose for my life. Enable me to concentrate on that which is right and proper. Let me not give in to petty squabbling or bickering. I place my reputation and that of my loved ones into your hands. Do what you will with us and let us live our lives to bring honor to your name alone. Give me today the grace to respond with loving-kindness. Help me overlook the offences of others. And teach me how to see past the hurtful remarks intended to unfairly influence my choices. I open my heart once again to receive the goodness of your grace. Let my thoughts and my words evidence your redemptive work on the cross. And I pray that I will continue to strive toward pleasing you above all else. Today and every day, I want first and foremost to look to you for wisdom, guidance, and instruction. Amen.*

*We know that worry hurts us and those around us. We drop worry off at a prayer meeting but it stalks us home.*
—DAVID HANSEN IN *Long Wandering Prayer*

# 18
## Unfair Assumptions

$\mathcal{E}$llen sidestepped the cardboard boxes sitting next to her computer station. With one more box load of accounts receivable files still to unpack, Ellen's back already ached from stooping over the entire morning. Once these get re-filed, I'll be set to get busy on today's entries, she reflected. Gathering another large pile of old receipts, Ellen tripped as she turned the corner from her working area, and down they went. All of her multicolored paper-thin sheets flew helter-skelter all over the floor. Under her breath, Ellen chided herself for trying to carry too much at one time. Then she knelt down and started picking up the strewn files. Although it took some time, Ellen breathed a sigh of relief as she realized that the files weren't too disorderly. Still, this extra chore would put her behind schedule. And that's all I need, Ellen worried. Just get busy and make the best of it, she told herself.

As Ellen put her records in order, she found that one of her coworkers had mistakenly filed a stray account with Ellen's batch. She looked over the receipt and realized whose file she held. Well, if that doesn't beat all, Ellen shuddered; now I have to walk the entire length of the department and present this file to the last person who wants to speak to me. In the back of her mind, Ellen replayed the unkind remarks she'd overheard the first afternoon she entered the receivables department. Four, or was it five, of the Old Guard were making disparaging remarks about her before having ever met Ellen. She was stunned and their words stung. Even though it was true that her father held an executive position with the company, surely her associate's degree in business qualified her to work as a clerk. It was obvious to many in Ellen's department that they certainly didn't think so. Even after twelve months, Ellen's colleagues continued to shut her out at every opportunity. But Ellen had learned some valuable lessons observing her father's business dealings. And she knew from the get-go that giving up was not an option for her. Somehow she'd learn how to move onward and upward despite the opposition.

*For consider Him who has endured such hostility by sinners against Himself, so that you may not grow weary and lose heart.*
—HEBREWS 12:3

*Dear Lord, I am trying to find a way to put an end to the unfair treatment I've been receiving. Unlikely as it is, I'd love to appeal to those who oppose me with the truth. Lord, you know that I would never take advantage of others by grasping for either position or prestige not merited. I have done nothing wrong. And certainly I've done nothing to be ashamed about. Yet those around me seem to think differently. They truly believe that I have finagled my way into this place. They couldn't be more mistaken. I worked hard to prepare for this position. And if anything, I'm overqualified! Lord, help me make sense of this troubling situation. Lend me a large portion of both wisdom and insight. I need to look at this situation from another perspective. I cannot continue living in this manner. Everywhere I look, I imagine someone is speaking badly of me. I don't want to be paranoid, yet I've been on the receiving end of far too much ill will these past months. It has made me distrustful and wary. I admit I do not like the changes I see in myself. Will you help me overcome with your grace the obstacles that face me? Teach me to look beyond the pettiness and insincerity of others. Only with your unconditional support will I be able to return good for evil— and do so from a pure heart. Lord, I am wounded. But I do not want revenge. What I desire most of all is understanding, and perhaps the benefit of doubt. If I have in any way encouraged this negative behavior by either my attitudes or actions, please make it clear to me. I want my heart and my motives to be unselfish and right. Aid me in this quest, Lord. Enable me to love even those who desire my downfall. I look to you alone for comfort, strength, and the perseverance to do what is honorable in your eyes. Amen.*

*The safest people are those who don't have to know something, nor do they talk about what they do discover.*
—JAN SILVIOUS IN *Look at It This Way*

# 19
## Second Class

Kandi tried to ignore the remarks she overheard from the dining room. She continued steadily working around the kitchen preparing the holiday brunch, her gift to her frequently small-minded family. Keep busy, she told herself. Quit thinking about what they're saying and get your mind onto what you're doing. Try as she might, Kandi just couldn't block out the stray comments that drifted into her work area. Still, she tried to concentrate on the fresh fruit tray she was assembling to go along with the assorted sweet rolls and breads that had just come out of the oven. Kandi looked over her handiwork and was momentarily pleased. It looks delicious, she admired. Once her quiche finished baking, the entire ensemble would be ready for devouring by her guests. But, Kandi wondered, would she be ready and willing to extend the olive branch of peace to her predominantly male family? Lord, help me, Kandi cried inwardly. I want to love them, I really do. But how can I get past their sexist comments? Time and again they have undermined my accomplishments and belittled my successes with their cutting remarks. It hurts too much to simply shut out. After all these years, and despite all good sense, my father and brothers still think women are no good for anything but cooking, cleaning, and bearing children. It isn't right, and their callous and malicious attitudes only reinforce the wedge already between us.

Taking a deep breath, Kandi offered up another silent plea for the good grace to treat her family with the respect she'd always hoped they would return. Although she didn't expect anything to change, Kandi made a commitment to continue paving the way for her loved ones to "see the light" by loving them despite their prejudices. She didn't often see this narrow-minded group, but when she did, Kandi determined she'd kill them with kindness at every opportunity.

*Bearing with one another, and forgiving each other, whoever has a complaint against anyone; just as the Lord forgave you, so also should you.*
—COLOSSIANS 3:13

*Dear Lord, can it be that I am still fighting against my loved ones' misplaced ideas and ignorant assumptions? Will it ever end? I wonder. All these long years I have tried to get them to see the error in their thinking. But to no avail. Nothing I say or do seems to make a whit of difference. Perhaps I am not the best person to offer such insights; after all, I have often responded with short-tempered retorts in answer to their ridiculousness. Still, as a woman of faith, I do desire recon-ciliation and peace to exist between us. My heart, despite feeling wounded, is still tender toward my family. I want to be an influence of godliness toward them. Yet I wrestle with my own insistent urges to strike back and inflict some well-deserved verbal lashings. I know this is not pleasing to you. I also believe that your principle of overcoming evil with good is the only option I can cling to. I have no choice if I want to seek the path you would have me travel. Lord, this is so very difficult for me. I admit that my pride sometimes clashes with my good sense. I want to punish those who have demeaned me. Yet you call me to a higher standard. You want me to love unconditionally. Help me begin again this day, fresh from time with you, renewed in both body and spirit, to be ready, willing, and able to extend love where it is most needed. Give me your grace and walk with me as I make yet another feeble attempt to give a blessing to those so needy in heart. I am your woman, confident and sure of my value and worth. And I thank you for the strength you've bestowed upon me. Amen.*

*You will change when instead of cursing you have learned to bless. It is one thing to try to stop cursing; it is quite another to start blessing. Cursing (inward and outward) will cease when blessing (inward and outward) truly replaces it.*
—JAY E. ADAMS IN *How to Overcome Evil*

# 20
## Out of Bounds

When Trish accepted the teaching position at her city's middle school, she was delighted to learn she could also sign on as the girls' assistant volleyball coach. Maybe this move will be better than I expected, Trish considered cheerfully. As Trish moved from room to room in her new, older home, she tried to figure out where to fit all her belongings. After being "downsized" from her previous position as a consultant, Trish went back to school and completed the needed courses to obtain her teaching certificate. Last spring's student teaching had gone so well that Trish wondered why she had waited so long before entering into this field. As an experienced volleyball player, Trish was in a good position to begin a part-time coaching job too. The biggest benefit of coaching was that Trish's daughter, Lindy, would play on the team and they'd spend some needed time together. Enough of the happy thoughts, Trish told herself, get back to work.

As Trish continued to mentally place her furniture around the rooms of the house, Lindy rushed into the room. "Can we invite the team over for a pre-season party like the one my other school had?" Lindy pleaded. "We'll see," Trish replied hesitantly. "Now let's get to work and get these boxes into the right rooms." Reluctantly, Lindy complied, and Trish allowed her mind to wander to the not-so-happy time the two of them had undergone at their previous residence. Trish would never forget Lindy's tear-stained face as she wept bitterly after being called unrepeatable names by a few of the neighborhood boys. Trish had tried to explain to Lindy that some people simply couldn't or wouldn't accept others who looked different from them. When the cutting remarks and ostracizing didn't stop, Trish decided to move to another area of town. It will be a new start all around, she told Lindy, a new job for me, a new school for you, and a new house for the both of us. Trish now believed she had made the best decision possible, it was just too bad that she'd been forced to leave one neighborhood simply because she was in the minority. But I won't stoop to their level, Trish determined. "Lindy, come here, I think we will have that pre-season party after all."

*And let us not lose heart in doing good, for in due time we shall reap if we do not grow weary.*
—GALATIANS 6:9

*Dear Lord, I come before your throne and I am calmed. I am at peace within my heart and soul. I know that you are continually interceding on my behalf and I thank you for that sweet assurance. This past season of my life has been difficult at best. You alone are aware of how afraid and confused I was. When the changes arrived, I wasn't sure how or where to proceed. But you directed me. Then, when I needed to make another monumental decision, you led me to a safe place. Thank you for guiding me through these uncertain times. I praise you for your goodness and faithfulness. My heart is overwhelmed by your trustworthiness.*

*Now I must come in petition of another sort. I ask that you lead my child and me to those who might accept us. Please direct me once more to people we might befriend. We have already endured the pain of rejection and spiteful antagonism. I feel as though we've had more than our share of ridicule. Lord, I never want to walk that path again. I am afraid of how I might react should I ever be placed in such a demoralizing situation again. Will you give me the strength to put the pain of the past into the past? Will you undertake for me even now and enable me to let go of the heartache I still occasionally feel? I want to press ahead and expect good things of people we'll be meeting in the coming days and weeks. But I find myself hesitant and perhaps jaded because of what we've experienced. Lord, give us the strength to forge ahead and look for the positive. Never allow the sins of others to spoil the loving responses you desire us to extend, whether they deserve it or not. Amen.*

*Jesus Christ hates the sin in people, and Calvary is the measure of His hatred.*
—OSWALD CHAMBERS IN *My Utmost for His Highest*

# 21

# Estrangement

$\mathcal{E}$ yeing the clock on her desk, Gloria tried not to worry. She wrote out some bills, checked her daily calendar, and reorganized a desk drawer. Throwing away a few odds and ends made the time pass more quickly. But not fast enough for Gloria. Those small tasks out of the way, Gloria glanced at her wristwatch and sighed. Only another twenty minutes or so and the long-awaited visit with her grandson should begin. Before Gloria could consider the repercussions of the next thirty minutes, the telephone rang and she jumped. I wonder who's calling? Should I answer or not? She fretted. Gloria didn't take time to ponder; she picked up the receiver and greeted the caller with a tremulous voice. Responding with simple pat answers seemed wisest, Gloria thought, at least under these circumstances. "No, it's fine. I'm not angry, just disappointed. Maybe we can reschedule for next Saturday?" Gloria queried. "Goodbye then."

Hanging up, Gloria's hand shook and she inadvertently dropped the hand-held phone off its cradle and knocked it over. As the phone hit the wooden floor with a loud crack, Gloria shuddered. Not again, oh, no, not again. It's too much to take, this getting my hopes up only to dash them. Lord, I really cannot continue playing this game any longer. But what options do I have? I want to see my grandson. It's been months since my ex-daughter-in-law has allowed me any time with him. My darling little guy must have changed so much by now, I wonder if he'll even remember me. Gloria reached down, replaced the receiver, and decided she needed something to soothe her jangled nerves. Herbal tea? Sounds good. Heating the water, Gloria picked out her favorite teacup, a gift from her beloved grandson last Christmas. Fingering the festive moose designs on the side of the cup, Gloria realized how much had changed in one short year. She knew how her former daughter-in-law fought her wayward son's decision to divorce. Gloria also realized that perhaps her daughter-in-law, who was still reeling from the separation, might find it too difficult to face her yet. Memories can be powerful allies or terrible enemies, Gloria thought resignedly. The best thing I can do for them is to give her the time and space she needs and not add to her pain by judging her.

*He heals the brokenhearted,*
*And binds up their wounds.*
—PSALM 147:3

*Dear Lord, will you help me nurture the attitudes that you desire me to embrace? I am struggling now with such conflicting thoughts and emotions. On the one hand, I am feeling such sympathy for my hurting loved ones. On the other, I am running short on patience. I understand that the circumstances are troubling and have been hideously painful. But I feel the repercussions of this breach as well. I, too, am hurting. So I am fighting against this pity-me mentality. Lord, I believe you would have me set aside my own discomfort and reach forth with a heart ready and willing to minister healing and reparation. I would love to do so, yet the situation has not allowed me this option. Help me be stalwart in my commitment and let not my loyalty waver despite the setbacks I must endure. Give me the grace I require to get past my own disappointments, and do not allow my expectations to cause me to withdraw in like manner. I am eager to extend a loving touch. Will you open this door for me? Begin a new season of trust between my family and myself. I sit here, quietly waiting for you to act as you see fit. Encourage my careworn heart with the eternal truths found in your word. Let my soul be filled with joy again. And I pray that I would learn to relinquish my dearest hopes to your perfect will. I commit my family into your care and keeping, believing that you will transform even this tragedy into something good beyond my imaginings. Amen.*

*If spiritual maturity is one's goal, it seems to me that praying for blessings for oneself is something of a backward approach. . . . He [Jesus] prayed, rather, to do his Father's will. Jesus said we must deny the flesh, not indulge it with prayers that continue to feed it.*
—MICHAEL PHILLIPS IN *Make Me like Jesus*

# 22

## *Under Duress*

When Leann moved back home to live with her elderly mother, she expected to make some adjustments, work through a few skirmishes, and just generally have to give in to her mom's preferences. But Leann had never anticipated the outright resentfulness that marked her mother's every comment. From the time her mom came out of her bedroom in the early morning hours to late every evening, Leann bore the brunt of her mom's legacy of bitterness. Leann dreaded hearing her mother's footfalls anymore. What to do? Leann had tried to point out the bright side of life to her mom. She attempted to overcome the prevalent air of negativity that hung so heavily in the house with small acts of kindness and little gestures of generosity. Yet nothing worked. It didn't matter what tack Leann took, her mother was seemingly determined to see life as a glass half-full, or not even that.

Leann had always been able to handle her mom's dark moods in the past, but that was before she lived with her. Now Leann found herself fighting the same oppressive spirit of negativity that her mother clung to so desperately. Leann wondered whether she had made a terrible mistake moving home. In retrospect, Leann realized she had made the decision after careful consideration and prayer, then why did it feel like God had abandoned her in such a desolate circumstance? With no ready solutions, Leann decided to give it a full year before making any other arrangements. Once Leann determined to overcome the foe of defeatism, she made a battle plan. Regardless of how her mother opted to live out her last days, Leann poised herself to lean heavily on God's grace and power to live her life with a positive, contagious confidence.

*And my God shall supply all your needs according to His riches in glory in Christ Jesus.*
—PHILIPPIANS 4:19

*Dear Lord, can I admit to you how extremely dejected I feel at this moment? Somehow, just sharing my struggles with you encourages me. My load is lighter, my burden not so overwhelming. Thank you for listening to my frequent prayers of complaint. I do not believe I could have lasted even this long without your constancy and care for me. Despite my most earnest efforts, I continue to battle against a lifetime's worth of negativity and defeatism. Lord, I never realized how captive my loved one was to this disease of the soul. It grieves me. It also angers me as well. I believe I have given my best to encourage this hurting soul to let go of the blackness and embrace the light of your love. Yet nothing has worked. Still, I cling to your promises of provision. Day by day, I will come before your throne with a prayer of entreaty for assistance and aid. Hour by hour, I will petition you for grace to love sincerely and the self-control to speak with wisdom. Put a new reserve of hope within my failing spirit, Lord. Teach me how to live with one so disagreeable and let me not be overcome by another's sin. Place a guard around me and protect me even in the midst of such turmoil. Let my life be a witness of your redemptive power to this wounded one. I understand that I am not able to handle such stress in my own strength. Rather, I have learned just how feeble my attempts at bringing about change truly are. Lord, I confess that I have wanted to toss in the towel and give up. But a small part of me wonders if I am justified in doing so. Your word promises that good can come from even the most disastrous of circumstances. Will you make it so even for us? Strengthen my faith and my resolve. Enable me to continue pressing ahead, and give me the vision to see past the predicament I am in. Burden my heart with a love so resilient that I am compelled to stay the course despite any personal discomfort. For the sake of your son and his sacrifice, I pray these things. Amen.*

*Looking ahead, it seems like a lifetime, but looking back, it's just the blink of an eye.*
—God's Little Devotional Journal for Women

# PART THREE

# In Sickness and Health

The human body is a marvelously intricate machine that needs meticulous attention and care to keep it running at its best. Yet even with the most conscientious preventive measures, the human body breaks down, contracts illnesses, and sometimes fails to rally with even the finest medical intervention. Death enters the equation and adds yet another dimension to one's ability to cope during this emotionally demanding season. Everything seems bleaker in the midst of such periods. Yet God has promised sufficient strength for every occasion, available for the asking.

# 23
# Never Good-Bye

Corey sat on the bed next to her twenty-one-year-old daughter Molly. She stroked her daughter's hair and rubbed Molly's favorite body lotion over her frail arms, legs, and feet. She urged Molly to drink another sip of water. Corey spoke softly, describing in intricate detail, at Molly's insistence, all the Christmas gifts she'd been purchasing for family and friends. Corey had just finished setting the scene for the early morning holiday breakfast when Molly drifted back off to sleep. She prayed that Molly might get enough rest in this single stretch to feel somewhat more alert the remainder of the afternoon, but she doubted that would happen.

Training herself to forge ahead despite the inevitable, Corey was having a difficult time of it. She wondered how she would muster up the strength to continue living, knowing full well that her daughter was dying. Sent home to die, isn't that when hospice enters the picture? Corey still reacted with physical revulsion every time she allowed her thoughts to stray toward that dangerous place. And at two this afternoon, Corey would be faced more directly with death than at any other moment in the past six months. When the hospice worker arrived to meet Molly and the family, Corey would have to pull together and put on the brave face one more time for Molly's sake. Tears threatening, Corey's heart cried out. How could this be happening? My beautiful, vibrant daughter, dying? Corey felt as though Molly was already beyond her reach, her aid, because they both knew Molly's strength was ebbing away by the hour. There would never be another special celebration for Molly, not in this life. Corey closed her eyes and blocked out the cacophony of noise inside her brain. I'm so afraid, Corey admitted, not for Molly, but for me. Will life ever hold any meaning for me again once she's gone? If Molly had the energy to do it, she'd be shaking some sense into me right this minute, telling me she wants me to go on living and live richly for her sake.

*Have I not wept for the one whose life is hard?*
*Was not my soul grieved for the needy?*
*When I expected good, then evil came;*
*When I waited for light, then darkness came.*
*I am seething within, and cannot relax;*
*Days of affliction confront me.*
*I go about mourning without comfort;*
*I stand up in the assembly and cry out for help.*
—JOB 30:25–28

*Dear Lord, I doubt if I will even be able to hold it together long enough to offer up a prayer that makes any sense. My thoughts are all in a jumble. My emotions are either raging or eerily dormant, and my soul is pained beyond telling. I wish there was some respite from this hideous reality. I long for just a few moments of peace to envelop me, to take me away from the hurt. But there is no magical destination to which I can travel, no surreal place that will lift this burden from my shoulders. Indeed, if there were, I would not go. My place is here, in the midst of my worst nightmare. I must not abandon my loved ones to suffering alone, even if I fear it more than they. I cannot say how overpowering this ordeal has been to me. Exactly how does one watch another die? Is it even possible to do so without permanent repercussions? I wonder.*

*Lord, I am feeling alone and doubt that I will ever recover. I cannot imagine a time when pain will cease to be my closest companion. Perhaps I do not wish it to leave me. Somehow, I find it comforts me. I know this sounds strange, but I would be forfeiting a significant part of me if I ever fail to look back without some measure of grief. Oh Lord, will you intercede for me now? I am lost. I am at your mercy. Light my way with the singular flame of your constant love. Direct my path and speak truth to my soul. Amen.*

*People have asked me if in hindsight it was really that bad. My honest answer: Yes. It was far worse than words can convey. Yes . . . but God is good. When I faced that horrible year, I honestly believed it would destroy me. Now I have perspective. It was a huge, destructive hailstorm in an otherwise very blessed life.*
SHARON MARSHALL WITH JEFF JOHNSON IN *Take My Hand*

# 24

## Easy Does It

In the basement-workroom of their home, Renee ran a successful soap-making enterprise. What had started out as a hobby for Renee eventually grew into a nice little business endeavor. Renee had been employed as a scheduling secretary for a pediatric surgical team for many years. Then a car accident precipitated major back problems for Renee. No longer was a desk job an option for her, as the incessant pain made Renee's life miserable. After two operations and endless months of recovery and eventual rehab, Renee's surgeon finally admitted partial defeat. "You'll have to live with some of the pain for the rest of your life," he told Renee regretfully, "but there are some tricks we can do to help." One of those "tricks" included restricting the time Renee sat down each day by rotating her tasks with a deliberate routine that bordered on obsessive.

The last thing Renee wanted to do was quit her job, but at this juncture, the pain often became so intense she couldn't carry out her responsibilities. So Renee and her husband brainstormed the idea of her starting up a home business where she would have the flexibility to be up and about and moving around. Two years hence and Renee's one-time hobby now brought in a tidy supplemental income. Renee still fought the pain on a daily basis but it was manageable. Then one pre-holiday evening, a sudden storm took their power out while Renee was busy packing up orders. Bustling over to the circuit breaker, Renee slipped over some packing materials and fell flat on her back. Unimaginable pain soared through her body, and she screamed. Hours later and under mild sedation, Renee could partly make sense of the grim news that another operation had been scheduled to repair the damage. Renee closed her eyes, thinking back to the long road to recovery she'd already been down twice, and despaired. Feeling the tears seep out of her tightly shut eyes, Renee felt alone until another firmer hand grasped her own and held it tight. She looked up and saw the fierce determination in her husband's eyes. He wouldn't let her give up.

*Listen to Me in silence,*
*And let the peoples gain new strength.*
—ISAIAH 41:1

*Dear Lord, you are my God, my comfort, and my source of strength. You alone are able to transform the suffering of this world into reason for rejoicing. Let it be so with me even now. I pray that you would take my wounded heart and my feeble, ravaged body and remake me into a vessel fitted with strength enough to serve. I cannot tell how discouraged I am. I am despondent. To think that I must traverse the same path of pain I've already traveled is insufferable. You, of course, know my thoughts. Nothing escapes your notice. Still, I feel as though I am traveling this weary road all alone. I know what the coming days hold for me, and the outlook is not pleasant. But walk this road I must. I beg for your mercy, your touch of compassion upon me. Strengthen my resolve to focus on getting better. Give me courage when I falter and hide me within the shadow of your wings when I am afraid. Let me keep my eyes always upon my goal. Make up for my lack in every area and continue to gently guide me to the other side of this treacherous condition.*

*I admit to feeling undone and overwhelmed by the prospect of what lies ahead. Will you banish my fears and cast them far from me? Keep my heart and soul safe within the bounds of your love. I do offer my most heartfelt thanks and praise for the countless ways you have faithfully blessed my life. I believe that you are for me, not against me. Help me set this truth ever before my mind's eye. I commit my life into your care, trusting fully in the goodness that you have demonstrated so abundantly, despite my frequently wayward heart. Teach me how to sing your song of praise as I make this journey by faith alone. Amen.*

*I am grateful for sight and sound and breath. If ever in my life there is a pouring out of blessings beyond that, then I will be grateful for the miracle of abundance.*
—ANDY ANDREWS IN *The Traveler's Gift*

# 25
## Golden Years

At seventy-three, Beth, a lifelong single lady, relished her quiet time. Ever since her father had died some thirty years ago, Beth had lived alone. Neat, tidy, and extremely precise pretty much summed up the way Beth liked to run her home. She had frequently, and sometimes almost callously, boasted to friends and neighbors that she would never end up in a nursing home. Beth had an aversion to so many sick, elderly folks, especially the sick ones. Having enjoyed robust health for most of her long life, it was no small surprise that when Beth was diagnosed with colon cancer, she was stunned and badly shaken. After making the necessary arrangements, Beth reconciled herself to a few weeks in the local hospital followed by respite care in a nearby rehabilitation facility. Beth put on a brave face and pressed ahead. Following her surgery, she finally realized just how ill she really was. She couldn't get out of bed, couldn't use the bathroom, and couldn't even reach for her eyeglasses without asking for assistance.

Beth was getting what she later termed a crash course in humility. Day by day, Beth did continue to grow stronger. Her cancerous tumor had been contained, and the surgeon felt confident Beth would recover completely. Still, Beth had a long road to living independently again. Days stretched into weeks before her great nephew drove her home on a sunny summer afternoon. Now using a walker, Beth carefully made her way into her kitchen. The following days were filled with visits from health care workers, nurses, house-cleaning help, and supportive friends and neighbors. Beth had stabilized physically, but she continued to fight battles that waged against her sense of mental well-being. Interminable what-ifs plague her mind. At night, Beth waged another sort of battle. Fear tormented her and she fought against unseen enemies until dawn. Late into one particularly difficult night, Beth decided to turn on the TV. Flipping through the channels, she hit upon a youngish woman singing a song of praise that went straight through Beth's doubting heart. For the remainder of that solitary evening, Beth continued to sing in her heart, and very slowly the song in her soul began to blossom and thrive.

*Therefore we do not lose heart, but though our outer man is decaying, yet our inner man is being renewed day by day.*
—2 CORINTHIANS 4:16

*Dear Lord, you know my struggles better than I can express them. I've always been able to care for myself. My entire life I've been the one who has taken care of other people. Everyone seemed to look to me for help. And I've never minded tending the needs of my friends and family. But how do I now adjust to being completely dependent on strangers?*

It goes against everything I am to ask for support from outsiders. Have I been prideful? Am I too independent?

Lord, please work within my heart. Give me flexibility not to fight against the circumstances you allow to come into my life. Let me see the good even in the worst scenarios. I am so set in my ways, Lord, I'll need all the grace you can bestow on me to overcome my self-reliance. Teach me how to accept a helping hand when it's offered. And please help me sleep at night. I'm so torn up with worries about getting sick again. I'm not resting at night, and I feel spent before I even get up. Lord, I know that you are continually at work transforming me into the image of Christ. Never stop this great task, but please give me your good hand of strength to see me through these trials. I want to be all you desire me to become. I'm finally seeing that I cannot do this alone anymore. Thank you for showing yourself faithful to meet my every need. My faith has grown stronger because of your goodness. And my future, be it a long one or one cut short by sickness, is in your hands as well. Minister to me in my weakness and buoy me up with your hand of compassionate provision. Amen.

*The struggles are not a mistake. They are tokens of redemptive love. Trials should not lead us to doubt the love of the King; they should convince us of it.*
—PAUL DAVID TRIPP IN *War of Words*

# 26

## Time Out

Denise checked the medicine bottles on the cupboard and began counting the pills in each one. Since her elderly father's Alzheimer's had taken a firmer hold on his ever-depreciating memory, Denise wanted to be certain her dad hadn't taken his pills already. Normally, she locked the meds away and dispensed them herself, but Denise needed to run errands and her mother promised to keep Dad away from the kitchen while she was out. Not surprisingly, Denise's father usurped her mom's authority and did what he wanted despite her protests. Denise later learned that Dad had been puttering around in the kitchen the entire two hours she'd been away. Her mother, recently diagnosed with Parkinson's, was no match for the still physically robust man, so she demurred and let him have his way.

Denise had come home to a crying, distraught mother and an angry, resolute father. And to beat all, both were upset with her! Her father ranted and raved that he was still capable of caring for himself, thank you very much. Her mother just cried and held her right arm tightly to her side to stop the tremors. A part of Denise died every time she looked at her parents and saw them slowly deteriorate in both mind and body. Another part of Denise felt upset that all her sacrifice and hard work went unappreciated. She tried to stop the wave of resentment that seemed part and parcel of every day lately. Denise wanted to help her parents in their later years. Instead, she found herself crumbling under the heavy weight of such a task. Life at home with Mom and Dad wasn't turning out as she'd hoped. Frequently, Denise was fighting with her parents as she attempted to give them the very care they so needed but were unwilling to receive. Denise knew that in her current state of mind, she'd soon need some medical care, too. So she determined to find new ways to take care of her loved ones without jeopardizing her own health.

*Let us hold fast the confession of our hope without wavering, for He who promised is faithful.*
—Hebrews 10:23

*Dear Lord, when I consider the place where you have me now, I am troubled and comfortless. I do not see any good in my being present in such a dismal environment. Help me gain new bearings on this decision I've made. Enable me to better understand why I'm here. Lord, I would like nothing better than to turn back the hands of time and choose differently. As I look back, I honestly believed I was making the wisest decision possible. Didn't I look at this proposition from every angle? Didn't I understand what sacrifices would be expected from me? Didn't I grasp just how difficult daily life would be as caretaker and guardian? Yes, I did anticipate all of the above. Still, I find myself lacking the strength to endure. I am not the strong and resilient woman I once believed I was. This revelation, too, haunts me. For so many years, I have glibly assumed I would take over when the time came. Without much warning, this transition transpired, and I am left floundering around wondering if I've made a terrible mistake.*

*I realize that it is too soon for me to give up, though I long to do just that. So my prayer this day is for grace to endure and stamina to withstand the assaults that come my way. Give me the passion to serve regardless of my own comfort level. Remake my often stubborn heart into one that is both flexible and adaptable. As I continue to "hang in there" by the merest threads of faith, teach me to call upon you, my only true source of strength. Change me, Lord! Even if my circumstances remain grim, let the joy of your salvation rule over all. Amen.*

*When belief is gone, faith is gone, hope is gone, love is gone . . . what then? When God himself seems gone . . . what then? What then is this? It is time for faith to exert itself. Faith that cannot see . . . yet still wills to believe and arises and goes to the Father and cries, My God!*
—MICHAEL PHILLIPS IN *Make Me like Jesus*

# 27
## Tender Talk

It was mid-July and Gina was busily preparing some favorite dishes for her husband's family's annual summer get-together the following afternoon. At this large gathering of some seventy-five-plus immediate and extended family members, everyone would be there. Everyone wanted to be there—everyone except Gina's husband Don. Gina tried to put thoughts of Don on the backburner of her mind. She wanted to enjoy her afternoon of baking without thoughts of his lingering depression spoiling her own mood. But it wasn't that simple. Gina continued to work around the kitchen, setting out ingredients for her trademark coffee cake and cinnamon rolls. As she mixed the yeast and water together, the bubbles formed and Gina turned to measuring the sugar, eggs, and such. Reminiscing about happier, less complicated times, Gina felt like crying. Hadn't she wanted to throw in the towel countless times during the past ten years, too?

Certainly, Don's job loss had precipitated much of the heartache they now faced. Then Don's dad died suddenly and unexpectedly. That was another blow to Don's already fragile emotional state. And just this past week, Don had received the news that the job he'd applied for six weeks ago had been given to another man. Chalk up another disappointment for Don. Gina, who worked full-time at a local catering business, was beginning to lose patience with her hurting spouse. She was frustrated because all her attempts to help him hadn't worked. In fact, Don had told Gina flat out, "Stop trying to make things all better. After all, I'm not a child." At that remark, Gina had cried. *Lord, help me know how to best help him,* she prayed desperately. Thinking out loud, Gina began talking through her struggles as she rolled out the dough, and it helped. Though Gina would most likely be attending their reunion alone the next day, she was determined to do so with a positive, hopeful attitude. And, Gina decided, *I'll ask Don one more time if he'd like to join me. Maybe,* she mused, *it might help him to know that his presence is still desired.*

*Bear one another's burdens, and thus fulfill the law of Christ.*
—GALATIANS 6:2

*Dear Lord, I come before you this day, empty-handed, bereft of hope, and struggling to maintain my own sense of perspective. I admit that I've allowed myself to become mired in the same incapacitated state as that of someone I love. Though I have attempted to correct and cajole my dear one into a better state of mind, nothing I have tried has worked. Indeed, most of my efforts have contributed to yet more heartache. Please help me, Lord. I need your wisdom and good sense to know when to back off and allow my loved one to fight his own battles. There is only so much I can do to intervene. I understand that all of us must stand up to our own enemies of the soul and look to you for strength. Yet I long to stand alongside and bring reassurance and comfort as well. Will you give me a sensitive spirit, Lord? Enable me to step back and allow you to do the good work you desire in this person. Show me how to retreat from the battle even when I long for nothing more than to set everything aright. Make my heart both wise and compassionate. Let me see this problem through your eyes. Create in me a passion for passionate intercessory prayer, Lord. I believe that at this juncture, as I continue to plead for my loved one's needs before your throne, that this is all you are calling me to accomplish. Give me the stalwart faith to continue praying day in and day out, for however long it may take. I pray, too, that you continue to hold my beloved in the palms of your hands with a grip so fierce that nothing can step between the two of you. Again, I commit this situation into your care and your keeping, trusting in your power to bring genuine, lasting healing in your time. Amen.*

*We reach out to those we think need help, and in the process of giving that mercy, we ourselves are helped. Which is the great paradox about the life of encouragement.*
—JOHN SLOAN IN *The Barnabas Way*

# 28
## The Long Haul

Scouring the bathroom for the fourth time in two days, Ellie was spent. She scrubbed, poured, sprayed, and wiped numerous disinfectants and cleansers throughout the room and then worked her way through the rest of the house. She unmade the beds—again. Washed the linens, towels, and every article of clothing not currently being worn. She walked around spraying a floral disinfectant until her house smelled like a flower shop. Ellie was a woman on a mission. If there was any way to bring a halt to this particular intestinal virus, Ellie would gladly have attempted it. After this insidious illness had crept up on them unawares, she was determined to wipe out the virus before it wiped her out.

Ellie was disheartened when her husband came home sick earlier in the week; the following afternoon her son became ill. The next day, both of Ellie's daughters were on the run to the bathroom day and night. Ellie, exhausted from her duties as nurse and sterilizer, was wondering when it would hit her. She didn't think she could make it through another night without sleep. Ellie realized she'd soon succumb to the dreaded virus herself if she didn't get some rest. But how was that possible? With four family members down for the count, Ellie was it, the last survivor. She didn't have the luxury of resting right now. It hadn't been too bad for the first few days, but when one after another of her family fell ill, this stretch of the flu was starting to outlast even Ellie's normally resilient constitution. "Lord," she cried out, "I'm frazzled and frustrated and undone. Help me, please, give me the strength I need for today. I'm counting on you, every minute, every hour."

*Whoever serves, let him do so as by the strength which God supplies.*
—1 PETER 4:11B

*Dear Lord, it's another day, and I'm so weary I wonder how I'll summon up the energy to accomplish all that needs to be done. Throughout the night, and a very long, exhausting night it was, I was up and about making certain that my loved ones had what they needed. In all honesty, I wanted nothing more than to crawl into my own bed and cocoon myself under a pile of blankets. But I could not, would not do that. My family is in great need and they are hurting, so my options are few. Though I feel so limited by my own waning strength, I am counting on you to get me through. It seems to my exhausted body that we have been fighting sickness for a long while now, but it hasn't really been so many days, simply intense and draining ones. Lord, will you come to my aid now? Be with me this day as I make my way from patient to patient. Enable me to lift their burdens with the small comforts I can offer. Show me the most effective ways to ease the suffering around me. Let me bring a measure of encouragement and hope to them as well. I pray that each one be healed swiftly and that they might sense your comforting presence as they recover. Give me all that I require to serve them and you. I rely solely upon your generous portions of both strength and might. Let me not give in to discouragement or depressing thoughts. Help me see past this temporary setback and keep my eyes set upon you. I know that as tired as I am, it would be so easy to linger on the negative and allow my own spirit to wane. Lord, again, no one knows the frailty of my frame better than you, so please, extend your compassionate hand of resource to me even now. I have no other to go to, and I understand this well. Amen.*

*When you accept the fact that sometimes seasons are dry and times are hard and that God is in control of both, you will discover a sense of divine refuge, because the hope then is in God and not in yourself.*
—CHARLES R. SWINDOLL IN *Stress Fractures*

# 29
## Collision Course

When Karen finally dozed off in her rocker, her body drew in the much-needed reprieve. Rarely in the past several days had Karen been able to sleep much at all. Rather than experiencing the rejuvenation she so needed during the quieter nighttime hours, Karen was up and roaming the house, worrying about her son Andrew. As the rest of the family slept on, and Karen marveled that they were able to do so, the relentless uncertainty she battled never went away. True enough, Andrew's checkup from three months earlier had pronounced his cancer to be in remission. But Karen was wise enough to know that their appointment the following morning and the resultant tests might bring a completely different diagnosis. How she tried to suppress the memories from over two years ago, but Karen would never, ever forget the look on her son's face when the doctor gave them the sober news that Andrew had cancer. After weeks of chemotherapy and a surgery, Andrew's body had grown wan and frail. Karen often cried bitter tears in private. But Andrew had been resilient and soon regained his former strength.

Still, Karen's insides twisted whenever her thoughts drifted ahead to their next checkup, drawing closer on the calendar. She wanted to place the situation into God's hands and take her own off. But how was that possible? Karen spent hours pleading for her son's life and his complete healing. Were her fervent prayers being answered now? Would Andrew be among the statistics that beat this particular cancer? Karen felt a longing for some assurance, some promise, that their nightmare was a thing of the past. But she also realized that life was uncertain, no one is guaranteed a tomorrow. So while Karen continued to fight against her fears, she also entreated God for peace, his peace that would indeed pass all her understanding. And at last, Karen did indeed sleep.

*The Lord will fight for you while you keep silent.*
—EXODUS 14:14

*Dear Lord, I'm here once again, coming into your throne room and pleading like a beggar for your mercy and compassion. I can think of no other place where I might receive the strength I require to fight this battle that rages within me. I long for your touch of peace to surround me completely. My soul is crying out for some reprieve from this burden I carry. Somehow, I am convinced that until I am fully confident that my loved one is out of danger, I must not relent. I have a private vigil I must keep. Lord, I know that this is not reasonable. I am not strong enough to continue this battle in my own strength. But I feel compelled to do so. If not me, then who will combat the destructive forces that threaten my dear child? Lord, I am called by you to intercede in prayer for the needs of those around me. And pray I do. I never stop. Lord, show me how to live my life free from this anxiety and still continue to call upon you for aid. It seems that as I labor in prayer, I am constantly reminded of the battle we face long-term, and I am unable to appreciate the blessings given us today. Somehow, I must find a way to let go of this weight yet stay connected to you through prayer. Is this even possible? I am consumed by thoughts that rob me of simple pleasures you would have me enjoy. Help me focus upon your unchanging character, Lord. Let my mind rest easy because of who you are. Despite my ever-changing circumstances, I can be at ease knowing you are sovereign and that your love for my child surpasses my own. Into your hands, I once again place all that my heart holds dear, and I ask you for the courage to leave it there. Be my constant guide and confidante as I continue to seek for the good each day holds. I trust in you alone to meet my every need. Amen.*

*Suddenly I realized I was concentrating on the problem rather than the Problem Solver. I was "prayerworrying." I determined to stop.*
JEANNIE ST. JOHN TAYLOR IN *How to Be a Praying Mom*

# 30
## Wounds That Don't Heal

*L*ois drove to her son's house three afternoons a week to offer some respite care to her daughter-in-law, who had more on her plate than any mother of five could handle. It was the least Lois could do, spending a few hours on these afternoons caring for her thirteen-year-old granddaughter, Emily, while Emily's mom tried to get caught up on her myriad other responsibilities. Lois, admittedly, was nervous when she offered to sit with her granddaughter after Emily's accident. Although she longed to be of assistance, Lois wasn't sure she could remember all the details of caring for Emily's special needs now.

As Lois continued on her way through town, she thought about that winter evening when she had received the call that Emily had been in a car wreck. And wreck it was. Emily was a passenger with family friends whose van was broadsided by another driver. As it happened, Emily's side of the vehicle was hit square on, and her body had taken the worst abuse from the impact. Six long weeks in the hospital and now, only home for the past three, Emily was indeed recovering. But she still had a cast on her left leg and arm. Her ribs were healing but tender and sore. The bruises on her cheek were finally just faintly recognizable. Lois could hardly recall that horrendous night without tears coming to her eyes. It just about did her in when she was called to the hospital and was ushered in to see her beloved granddaughter. Even now, Lois sometimes awoke in the middle of the night covered in a blanket of sweat as she relived Emily's suffering. Lord, she would pray after these late night episodes, please help me put this nightmare behind me. Give me the courage I need to look ahead and not live in terror anymore. As Lois turned into the driveway, she gathered her purse and bag of goodies, something special for all of her grandchildren, and silently asked God to use her to bring comfort, solace, and encouragement to those she loved so much.

*And if you give yourself to the hungry,*
*And satisfy the desire of the afflicted,*
*Then your light will rise in darkness,*
*And your gloom will become like midday.*
—ISAIAH 58:10

*Dear Lord, I come before you again to intercede for my loved one who is in such agony. I cannot bear to contemplate all that she has already suffered. It pains me to even consider the loss she has endured. Lord, will you come quickly now and bring your healing balm to her body? I ask that you stay close by and never wander from this one I care for. Please show yourself strong on her behalf. Be her rock of strength and her most gentle comforter. Enable her body to knit itself back together and heal every wound through the power of your intent and word. Let each new day bring renewed vigor and energy. And keep defeat at bay. Lord, I admit that I am feeling undone by this event. It has made me step back and live in fear, wondering when yet another such tragedy may befall my loved ones. Lord, I know this is not good. You would have me walk beside you with complete confidence in your perfect provision. Help me to do so now. Give me all I require to lend a helping hand and an encouraging word to my dear ones who are suffering so greatly now. I pray that my every word speaks of promise, hope, and bright expectancy for the future. Use me, Lord, to bring good into the lives of those around me. And surround my heart and mind with your protection and assurance. I desire nothing more than to ease the pain I see around me. Lord, will you make me able to do so? I offer myself to you today. Use me as a conduit of your tender love even now. Amen.*

*At the end of your days, be leaning forward—not falling backward.*
—H. JACKSON BROWN JR. AND ROSEMARY C. BROWN IN *Life's Little Instructions from the Bible*

# 31

## Service with a Smile

Serving up the chowder to her family, Joan was careful to set aside an extra-large helping for her neighbor Glenn. Whenever Joan was able, she made certain to put some food back for their ailing friend and neighbor. Joan thought about Glenn often these days. If she wasn't running back and forth to help him out with this or that, she was making telephone calls for him and running him to his doctor's appointments. And Joan didn't begrudge offering her time to Glenn, except when her own family's needs got in the way. Like any wife and mom, Joan felt she must meet the needs of those under her own roof first and foremost. After these most important commitments were fulfilled, Joan gladly stepped in and did what had to be done for Glenn. A widower, Glenn had had a rough few months since he fell while removing leaves from the eaves trough of his roof. Joan's husband had been working around their yard, saw Glenn's tumble, and ran to his rescue. Everyone was thankful that his broken ankle was healing nicely and he'd soon be able to resume his activities. But until Glenn's cast came off, he simply wasn't able to get around well enough to manage three daily meals, laundry, and cleaning chores. Joan realized this and tried to include Glenn on her daily calendar. Still, some days it was all Joan could do to zip in and quickly peruse the situation before dashing back out and onto the next task. Like today.

Once Joan and her family finished eating, she packaged up the meal and took it next door. Inside, Glenn and two of his buddies who had stopped by for a visit greeted Joan. As Joan looked on, she suddenly realized that these men, these good friends of Glenn's, were both hale and hearty. Why, she wondered, haven't they been willing to help Glenn, too? Trying to stifle an urge to ask them point-blank if they'd be around the next afternoon to run Glenn to his appointment, Joan gulped back the temptation. Saying her good-byes, Joan took her time walking across the dark lawn. Simmer down, she told herself, they just haven't given it any thought. Don't get all upset about something you can't control. Just do your part and let go of the rest.

*Examine me, O Lord, and try me;*
*Test my mind and my heart.*
—PSALM 26:2

*Dear Lord, I'd like to believe that I am always ready, willing, and eager to serve the needs of those around me with no thought of repayment. But it isn't so. I am so grievously tempted to flaunt the good works I have accomplished to virtually anyone who will listen. This is such a shameful truth; I am loath to admit it even to you, Lord. I found myself tempted to make a list of all that I do for the sole benefit of gaining appreciation earlier today. I wonder how long I will walk this earth before I recognize the foolishness of such ideas? Where do I get these selfish inclinations? It seems as though as soon as I do something in service for another, I am waiting, longing even, for some tiny measure of thanks. Lord, I pray that you would cleanse my heart of such desires. Help me live my life in service to you alone. Set me free from the bonds of man's praise and approval. I ask you, Lord, for a pure heart. Remake me into a woman of faith, strength, and peace. Let not minor interruptions dampen my spirit. Nor allow ever-changing circumstances to disturb my calm. I look to you, Lord, for all that I require. Please continue your work of refinement in my heart and soul. Be generous with your sustaining grace and let my portion be large! Teach me your ways and bind me close to you always. Above all, Lord, I want a good word from you. Amen.*

*Just as Mary knew that time with Jesus was more important than time for Jesus, the Lord wants us to understand that He desires our attention more than our energy—our time more than our timecard.*
—JEROMY DEIBLER IN *Far from Home*

# 32
# Best Guess

When Trudy came down the stairs with a load of laundry in her arms, she was startled to see her husband, Ron, sitting in their living room. She knew he'd left hours earlier for several important appointments, but she hadn't expected him to see him back this soon. "What happened?" Trudy queried. "How did your meeting go? Did they agree to release your funds yet?" Trudy had been praying all morning for Ron's tangled insurance and disability case to finally get sorted out. It had been several months since Ron's accident on the road, yet the promised financial recompense hadn't been released. It wasn't as though they were asking for a handout; certainly Ron's company understood that he hadn't planned on getting injured during one of his cross-country road trips. So what was the holdup? When would they receive the needed money for their daily living expenses? Ron's disability payment wasn't enough for them to make it on. Sure, they could pay their mortgage and a few utility bills, but until the company made good on their promises to intervene, it was touch and go in the finance department.

Not wanting to burden Ron any more, Trudy wished she could take back every one of her questions. Silently, Trudy stood there wondering what were they going to do.

Ron wasn't recovering as they'd hoped; he still wasn't given any release papers from his physician. And there was no way Ron's trucking firm would allow him back on the road without that precious release form. There seemed to be no way out, and each day their situation got bleaker. Trudy looked at her husband and felt a wave of compassion. *He's thinking the same thing I am. And he's overwhelmed and discouraged too,* she realized. *What have I been thinking. I'm not the one who's been injured and out of a job. Help me, Lord, to offer some timely encouragement right now.*

*In all labor there is profit,*
*But mere talk leads only to poverty.*
—PROVERBS 14:23

*Dear Lord, thank you for redirecting my concerns and fears to thoughts of you. I have been nursing a negative and defeated attitude of late. Seems like every day has brought more hardship and setbacks. I understand that the circumstances we are in are indeed bleak. But are you not the God who controls all? Have I forgotten that you alone are able to overcome any obstacle? Lord, forgive me for my lack of faith. I have neglected my much-needed time with you. Instead, I have allowed the trials of my day to rule over my better sense. I have given up without even coming to you for aid. Please make up for my weakness and frailty, Lord. Give me all that I need to stay the course you have set before me. Envelop me, both in mind and body, with your constant presence and reassuring hand of care. Lead us where we need to go. Open our minds to understand how to best traverse this path we're on. We are in need, that I freely admit. And we do not possess the wisdom or the insight to see how we will get through. But we trust now in your faithfulness and provision. We lift up our eyes and look to you for our every need. Lord, even now, will you renew our spirits with yours? Will you make us aware of your guiding hand that serves to support and strengthen us day by day? I pray that we falter no longer but live this day with grateful hearts, trusting hearts, looking only to you for what we require. Our lives may be out of our control, but with you by our side and standing with us, I am confident we'll see brighter days ahead. Again we commit our lives into your hands, waiting upon you for our deliverance, certain and sure that we will again praise you for even this time of trial and difficulty. Amen.*

*Faith is man's response to God's initiative. Your first faith was the positive response you made to the Holy Spirit when he brought truth about Christ home to your heart.*
—JOHN WHITE IN *The Fight*

# PART FOUR

## The Final Separation

Like most areas in life, there are counterparts. We laugh and then cry. We sorrow and then rejoice. We create life and eventually die. For some, the parting comes too sudden, too soon. Death abruptly robs us of a last good-bye or of a needed reconciliation. Guilt, anger, resentment, loneliness, or depression may follow. But if we've embraced God's gift of salvation, we can be certain and sure of where our eternity lies despite the ever changing circumstances surrounding us. And we can face our future with the hope of eternity propelling us forward.

# 33
## Unreachable

While Barb sat fingering her diamond engagement ring, she noticed it needed cleaning again. With a rueful expression, Barb wondered why that particular thought had even passed through her mind. *It doesn't matter now; I probably won't be wearing it much longer in any case.* Tears in check, Barb worked hard to maintain her composure as she sorted through her once-burgeoning list of wedding and reception details. She tossed away one reminder after another, reminding herself that she had to let it go and move on. After another half hour of such heart-wrenching labor, Barb was relieved to see she was almost finished. *I just need to clear out some extra bride's magazines I tucked in my desk and then I'll be done.* Gathering up the bulk of the final remnants of wedding paraphernalia, Barb stood by the garbage can and started ruthlessly pitching in one item after another. Feeling as though she'd accomplished more in one morning than in the previous few weeks, Barb sighed deeply: *now for a relaxing cup of coffee while I read the mail and paper.*

Concentrating on her task, Barb sat down at the kitchen table and looked through her mail. *Hmm, a letter from her aunt down south in Barb's hometown.* Curious, Barb retrieved the note from inside the envelope and out fell a newspaper clipping. Unfolding it first, Barb stifled a cry. It was their engagement photo, the one Barb's mom had sent in to the local paper. Barb noted the date, only seven weeks ago, when I was still happy, still counting the days until we'd be married. With a sadness so intense she couldn't see straight, Barb laid her head down and wept as she relived the morning when the call came that her fiancé had died in an accident. At the time, Barb had held together; she had done what needed doing while the rest of Pat's family and her own were crumbling around her. But now, some weeks later, it was Barb who needed strong shoulders to lean upon. And though she believed she was handling the tragedy well enough most days, Barb realized she'd still need the support of friends and family for a long time to come.

*The heart knows its own bitterness,*
*And a stranger does not share its joy.*
—PROVERBS 14:10

*Dear Lord, I am not handling this sad event too well. I thought I was doing all right. I felt like I alone was accepting this tragedy better than anyone else. But I was wrong. True enough, you gave me the strength to carry on and get through the first few weeks without falling totally apart. But now, in the quiet moments of my day when I have nothing to distract me from a future that will never be, I am coming apart.*

*Lord, I feel as though most of the time I do not even feel anything. I'm beyond the reach of my loved ones emotionally. It's as though I'm living in a vacuum. I'm alive and functioning, but the real me is hidden far, far away. I wonder when and if I'll ever feel alive again. Is it possible to love another person so deeply that their absence causes a grief too intense for healing? This, too, I think about. I admit I've done far too much solitary thinking lately. But no one else really understands what I'm going through. You alone are able to sift through the dross of my wounded heart and get to the real me. I don't want to forget this one I loved. I'm frightened beyond the telling of a future without this person by my side. Honestly, I don't want to face my life alone. I know that you are with me, but I want my loved one back, here, now. Lord, reach down to me, I beg. I cannot summon up the strength any longer to continue on. Help me now; I am counting on you, only you. Amen.*

*Confidence in God and hope in his provision do not, in this life, always reflect themselves in a breezy joy. Confident, hopeful people are marked by perseverance and a refusal to seek illegitimate relief in the midst of their ongoing struggles.*
—LARRY CRABB IN *Finding God*

# 34

## The Mourning Season

Joyce sped through the yellow traffic light en route to the shopping mall for a few last minute stocking gifts. Even though her sister's kids might be no-shows on Christmas morning, Joyce didn't want their Christmas stockings to look skimpy. Ever since Joyce's younger sister had been released from the hospital and placed into the care of hospice, Joyce's home had become the hub of all family activity. Months earlier, it had been at Joyce's where all the extended family had gathered to hear the news about Jodi's recurrence of cancer. A few weeks later, again at Joyce's, everyone got together to get a schedule in place for Jodi's caregiving while she underwent radiation therapy. And just days ago, at Joyce's kitchen table, they made the tough decision to bring Jodi home to die. This afternoon as Joyce went bustling from one store to another, she did a pretty fair job keeping her mind off of her sister's suffering. But those dreadful thoughts were always just below the surface, waiting for the slightest event to trigger another crying jag in Joyce.

Even though it was killing Joyce to watch her little sister waste away, Joyce wouldn't have had it any other way. She wanted Jodi in her home and close to her. But along with Jodi came Jodi's kids, three teens who had been jostled around from one extended family to another. With Jodi's ex-husband out of the picture and Jodi so very ill, it was left to Joyce and her siblings to open their hearts and homes to their niece and nephews. But all their do-gooding hadn't stilled the fury in these youngsters. They were angry, bitter, and ready to let fly at anyone who tried to get too close. So Joyce thought about small ways she could offer love of a tangible sort—ways that might not get so swiftly rejected. Stockings seemed innocuous enough, especially when filled with lots of goodies. As Joyce continued selecting the last few gifts, she prayed that God would use these tokens of love to break through the barriers of resistance and that maybe Jodi and her kids could relish one last holiday season together before Jodi passed away.

*Blessed are those who mourn, for they shall be comforted.*
—MATTHEW 5:4

*Dear Lord, I come before you in great anticipation and anxiety. I don't pretend to understand why illness and death come to some and not others. But I am struggling to maintain my peace of mind, actually any peace at all. It has been a long, exhausting road to walk these past months. And something in the very nature of witnessing someone young dying is against all reason. It just doesn't make sense to me. I try to step back and look at the situation from a detached perspective. Still, I'm left confused and confounded. Why not another? Why my loved one? Lord, I have to put this to rest somehow. I must accept the fact that my dear one will soon be gone. Will you help me, help us all get through these final days? I have so many unanswered questions, so many decisions to make as well. Please intercede for us now. Give us all the wisdom we require to make prudent and compassionate choices. And not only are we suffering along with our loved one, there are children to be considered. Lord, will you step in and minister your love and comfort to these youngsters? Let your constant presence bring healing to them. Soothe each one as the need arises. And take away fear of the future from their minds. Let them rest easy that they will be well loved and cared for.*

*As we all continue to journey toward death, stand with us and enable us to offer strength, assurance, and comfort wherever and whenever it is required. Let your enduring peace surround us and let us experience the joy of your surpassing love each moment of the day. Lord, only with your grace will we be able to conquer this foe we face. Be with us every hour. Amen.*

*Almost every trial increases our love for others. So even though we may not immediately see any other good, we know of at least one—more love.*

—GARY SMALLEY WITH AL JANSSEN IN *Joy That Lasts*

# 35
## Good Days

Feeling under the weather with a nasty cold and secondary sinus infection, Rachel had been lying low for the past two weeks. She had gone skiing with her kids, but only a day into their yearly trip she had been so stuffed up and miserable that she begged to stay in the condo and cozy up near the fire while her college-age kids snowboarded and skied. Rachel rested and sipped hot tea during the day, trying to salvage her strength for the evenings when they played board games and long Euchre tournaments. Their trip to their favorite ski lodge, Rachel's belated Christmas gift to her family, was over before she knew it. But she'd had precious time with each child, something she cherished more than ever since they were gone most of the year at their respective colleges.

Once home, Rachel made an appointment with her physician and was thankful to receive the prescription she needed to help clear up her full-blown infection. "A few more days will make all the difference," Rachel's doctor assured her. So as she settled herself on her couch with assorted books, magazines, bills, and letter-writing material, Rachel tried to make the most of her time. Weary of so many days of inactivity, Rachel's mind began to wander more and more. She pulled out her old photo albums and slowly perused each page. Some made her laugh, others cry. But every time she came to a picture of her deceased husband, Rachel felt a twinge of regret. Their marriage had been strong, they had loved their three kids, and Tom had had a wonderful job. Even after eight years, Rachel still couldn't understand how her husband had gotten so low that suicide had been his final choice. At the time, Rachel was devastated and her children, still in school, were awash in grief. But Rachel had taken stock of her own life and realized even then that Tom's choice would either kill her or make her stronger. She looked at her kids and opted for the latter. Even now, years later, Rachel still sometimes gave in to melancholy periods, but they never lasted. She refused to nurse those dark thoughts but determined instead to focus on a future bright with possibility and promise—and it had made all the difference.

*There is no fear in love; but perfect love casts out fear, because fear involves punishment, and the one who fears is not perfected in love. We love, because He first loved us.*
—1 JOHN 4:18–19

*Dear Lord, another beautiful moment with you, Lord, and I am ready to start my day. I am so at peace, my heart is full, and my life is blessed beyond my comprehension. I am filled with the joy that only arises from you. Thank you, Lord, for being to me more than a faithful friend or trusted confidante.*

*You are my savior, Lord, and God. How magnificent these truths are to me. But as I continue to bask in the goodness of your love, I can still recall a more difficult time. Not so very long ago, I was at a crossroads. There was no feeling of warmth or comfort, I felt so very alone and bereft of any solace. No one could share my grief—or so I believed. At my lowest point, Lord, you were there. Though I tried to dismiss your gentle, whisper-like nudging, you were persistent in your pursuit of me. How grateful I am that you did not let go of me. Your great love, though I did not understand or recognize it, was all that I needed. Looking back, I see it now. I was never alone and in your wonderful way, you drew me close to your side and comforted me. That was when I began to heal. Thank you, for loving me so. Mere words can never express the gratitude I feel. Yet I pray that with every lesson I've learned, you will bring increase in the form of good deeds, heartfelt compassion, and genuine love toward others who are hurting. I never want to forget the magnitude of your love. Amen.*

*When we're comfortable, we still need Him, but we don't feel that need as urgently. If there isn't much to motivate us to dive for pearls of truth, knowing God gets shoved to the bottom of our "to do" list—usually right below dusting the rafters in the garage.*
—SUSAN WILKINSON IN *Getting Past Your Past*

# 36
## Lost Opportunity

After Nancy unpacked the cluttered upstairs bedrooms, she started working through the downstairs of the home of her deceased neighbor and shirttail relation. One room at a time, Nancy either threw away or sorted through over eighty years of belongings. As a lifelong bachelor, Dan hadn't filled his old farmhouse with many valuables, but he been a kind soul who couldn't refuse a gift from any one of his many friends or neighbors. Nancy laughed more than once when she opened a drawer or a box and found the most hilarious items tucked away. Looking around her, Nancy realized she would be at this job for weeks before she'd see the end of it. No doubt, she realized, I'll continue to uncover even more "treasures" as I clear my way through the contents of Dan's home. Moving into Dan's bedroom, Nancy started with the small bedside table and pulled out the drawer. Full to the brim of old photos, newspaper clippings, and faded letters, Nancy couldn't help but stop and look through these more carefully. She often wondered why Dan hadn't married and started his own family. Perhaps she'd learn more about his past through the memorabilia he kept through the years. True enough, Dan had told Nancy he'd spent some years caring for his mother and then his father. As an only child, Dan felt responsible for his parents' care. Maybe he thought it was too late by the time his folks were gone, Nancy pondered.

Realizing she couldn't relegate these special keepsakes to the pitch pile, Nancy carefully put them into a box to take home with her. I'll look through them later and then decide where they need to go. As the executor and sole recipient of Dan's estate, Nancy knew full well there weren't any relatives to pass on these items to. Dan's only family had been Nancy and her children. Thinking back, Nancy felt good that she'd made it a priority to be available to help Dan whenever he needed it. Nancy also felt twinges of regret as well. She felt ashamed of the numerous times she complained silently after Dan had called for something. Lord, Nancy prayed, please forgive my selfishness. Even though Dan never knew what I was thinking at times, you knew.

*Do all things without grumbling or disputing.*
—PHILIPPIANS 2:14

*Dear Lord, I find myself torn between knowing that I served someone in need, doing all the right tasks and taking on whatever needed doing—on the outside. But in my heart, I have to admit I was shamefully resentful of the frequent expense in both time and energy that these small acts cost me. Lord, although no one knew what I was feeling apart from you, I still am experiencing significant periods of regret.*

*I wish I could turn back the hands of time and do it over. Please help me learn from my mistakes. I know enough about this life to understand that whatever I've faced once, I'll probably have to face again. I admit to feeling genuine grief over how I resisted being of service to my neighbor. It's true enough that I am already full to the brim with other responsibilities. But I wonder how you would have had me deal with these extra tasks? I am sure that your desire would have been for me to love a needy person with no thought to how I might be inconvenienced. In this way, I failed miserably. You desire not just a mere outward show of love but inward transformation of the soul. In hindsight, I feel so guilty. Lord, will you set me free from these entanglements? Help me set a new pace today, beginning now. Teach me to come to you quickly, without hesitation, so that I might find grace in time of need. And continue to remake me into one who delights in giving to others regardless of personal sacrifice. I know that only through the strength that you afford me will this ever come to pass. Amen.*

> *Our subordination of self to the love was, at least, a step towards the dying to self that is the inexorable demand of Christ. We sought the beautiful and perhaps the good, and we came at last to Messiah.*
> —SHELDON VANAUKEN IN *A Severe Mercy*

# 37
## Timeless

Meredith drove in the funeral procession following behind her parents' car. She had two of her own four children with her. The other two kids, along with her husband, were still packing up their belongings and cleaning the cottage they rented each summer. When news came of a fellow parishioner's death while they were vacationing, Meredith decided to come home early to attend the funeral. Another funeral. As Meredith trailed behind the hundred or so other vehicles bearing the telltale flag of bereavement, she wanted to cry and experience the release of her pent-up emotions. Instead, she felt only hollow inside. In a sad, morbid sort of way, Meredith realized she was getting pretty adept at handling such dire situations. How many friends and family members had actually passed away in the last eighteen months? Was it five or six? Meredith had honestly lost count. It was as though a rash of unexpected illness or accidents had been stalking those she loved.

Meredith recalled the first such episode. A lifelong friend of her family's had died of a heart attack. It was shocking, the grief intense. Then, an acquaintance had gotten into an accident that left behind Meredith's friend and a teenage daughter. A few weeks later, the son of a close friend had died, too. Next came the tragic news of her cousin's child's death. Meredith was especially shaken by this horrendous accident. It had caused her to step back and reassess her own faith. Life and its accompanying uncertainties were beginning to take its toll on Meredith's psyche. She found herself feeling anxious when her kids wanted to go out. She'd become fretful if they were late in arriving home. More than anything, Meredith wanted her peace of mind back. She considered how naïve she'd been. Did she really, honestly believe that the painful loss of life, an eventuality to all, would somehow pass by those she loved forever? Meredith knew better. But with all the recent reminders of death surrounding her, she understood that she'd have to work diligently to keep herself from succumbing to despair and hopelessness, and Meredith knew just where she'd find such resource.

*Put on the full armor of God that you may be able to stand firm against the schemes of the devil. For our struggle is not against flesh and blood but against the rulers, against the powers, against the world forces of this darkness, against the spiritual forces of wickedness in the heavenly places.*
—Ephesians 6:11–12

*Dear Lord, I am fighting against a foe far too great for me. I have become all too aware of the frailty of life these past months. I am learning a difficult lesson. Nothing is certain and life is not safe. It amazes me that I ever thought I could*

so order my path and my world to keep at bay all that
destroys life. I am indeed simple-minded. Lord, even now,
I sit and consider how many lives I have seen pass from this
world. It overwhelms me. Each dear soul was alive and well,
and then gone. How can I reconcile such events with the
knowledge that you are sovereign and reigning in heaven and
over earth? I stumble and falter when I attempt to come to
terms with such devastation. Yet I know that all must face
death. Life does not go on indefinitely. We must each one
choose how we will embrace our time on earth. And I do not
want to live my days as one fearful and anxious. Rather, I
make the choice to live my life by faith and on a foundation
set in place by your able and worthy hands. Lord, teach me
to be wise and to use my time in ways that bring help and
encouragement to others. Perhaps all the comfort I seek might
be more readily discovered as I labor to give comfort to others.
Be with me now, heal my broken spirit and renew me with
your strength. Give me the vision to see that the enemies
I fight against are not those of illness or accident but the
unseen forces that would rob me of my soul. I turn again
to you, desperate for your touch upon me. Amen.

> The incomprehensible God is made comprehensible through
> Christ Jesus our Lord. The unapproachable God is approachable
> only through Him.
> —ANN KROEKER IN *The Contemplative Mom*

# 38
## The Last Reunion

Jayne was ready to dash out the door to pick up her children from their summer camping trip. It had been two weeks, two long weeks, since she'd seen her twin boys. They had been making plans as far back as last winter to go hiking, hone their archery skills, and take an overnight canoe trip while at this particular camp's summer session. Jayne, like most other moms, gave them her cautionary lecture before she handed them their spending money. *At least I'll have their attention while I hold their cash,* she thought wryly. After saying their good-byes, Jayne drove back home and decided to make the most of her time without the boys. She'd already purchased paint for the kitchen and trim for the sills on their porch. Then she would tackle the boys' old game room to reorganize and toss out what they didn't need. She was also planning to take a couple of hours every morning to get her flower and vegetable garden into shape. Jayne felt energized and eager to jumpstart these summer projects.

And she held fast to her plans for the first week until she received a call from her mom that her younger brother, Seth, had been killed overseas. Jayne couldn't grasp the news. She had just received a letter from Seth a few weeks earlier. He was doing so well. Seth loved his most recent post as a weather forecaster, and he was even being considered for an instructor's position come the fall. Jayne mentally replayed the entire contents of Seth's last letter as she tried to get her mind around the fact that she'd never hear from him again. It was too much for her to make sense of. "How could this be happening?" she asked again and again. It didn't seem real. Perhaps if Seth had lived in Jayne's hometown and she'd seen him often, his death and subsequent absence might be more acutely felt. But none of the family had seen Seth in the last six months. They were used to his being gone. Now, Jayne realized, they would need to adjust to him never coming home.

*Rejoice with those who rejoice, and weep with those who weep.*
—ROMANS 12:15

*Dear Lord, I'm not quite certain how I should pray. Perhaps it is because my mind and feelings are still not able to grasp the loss I'm having to face. Will time aid me in this? Will conversation with loved ones better help me cope with this tragedy? I'm not sure. The only true hope I have for coming to grips with this is you. I believe that you are the one who will lead me through as I grieve this terrible loss. Always you have been my steadying rock of strength when life's obstacles have grown too great a challenge for me. Only with you by my side can I travel this rough and uncertain terrain. I admit to being shaken by these events. I take so much for granted. I'm ashamed to admit that I didn't often pray for my dear one. I was too busy living my life to sit down and quietly offer up petitions of prayer. I suppose I'm also feeling guilty—if only I'd prayed more for protection. Would this have made a difference? Lord, I understand that you hold life in your hands, so I must ask: Why didn't you keep this one I loved from harm? I don't even expect an answer, but I feel compelled to ask regardless. My heart is confused and my thoughts muddled. Lord, I ask that you bring clarity of mind and a renewed sense of purpose during these next weeks and months. Help me grasp what has occurred, and enable me to bring needed encouragement to the rest of my family. Teach me how to place my broken and bruised heart at your feet and allow you to heal me. Stay close with me, Lord. I need you. I must have your sense of peace to protect my heart and mind. Amen.*

*Jesus broke it all. Jesus supplied it all. The disciples gave it all. And the entire multitude was fed!*
—ANNE GRAHAM LOTZ IN *Just Give Me Jesus*

# 39
## The Heart Beats On

While Tammy waited her turn to be ushered into the examination room, she already knew the prognosis. Her unborn baby, at almost eight months, hadn't moved all night. With three previous pregnancies and births behind her, Tammy had instinctively sensed something was wrong. As Tammy tried walking around as a stimulus, she gently pressed her hand against her abdomen in an effort to prod her child into moving. But nothing. At first, Tammy had thought that her overactive imagination doing a number on her, causing her to worry when nothing was amiss. But after some very still hours, Tammy realized this wasn't something to dismiss. She called her obstetrician first thing in the morning and the doctor instructed Tammy to come to the office immediately. They'd do an ultrasound and check for a heartbeat. Certainly, Tammy thought in distress, they can do something.

As she continued to wait for her name to be called, Tammy grabbed her husband's hand tight and attempted to still the terrifying what-ifs that were thundering around in her mind. But try as she might, she already knew the truth. Her baby had died. Tammy didn't need anyone telling her that her once lively, unborn child had passed away. Something deep with Tammy already confirmed it. So

Tammy continued to sit, trying to still her own wildly beating heart. But it was no use, she could not endure the dreaded anticipation another minute, so she let go of her husband's hand and stood up, defiant and ready to march straight in to the inner sanctum and demand to be seen immediately. But before she had a chance to move, her husband got to his feet and took firm hold of Tammy and embraced her. As she leaned heavily against him, Tammy finally gave release to her emotions and wept freely. A nearby nurse quickly ushered the couple into a private room where both were able to offer what comfort they could to each other. When they were ready, Tammy was examined and then consoled by both her spouse and her physician, but as she cried tears of grief outwardly, Tammy never stopped crying out to God for help beyond the understanding of this world.

*And he shall wipe away every tear from their eyes; and there shall no longer be any death; there shall no longer be any mourning, or crying, or pain; the first things have passed away.*
—REVELATION 21:4

*Dear Lord, awakening this morning, after hardly having slept all night, I understood that the events of this day would forever alter my life. I was inwardly anticipating what might have already happened. In my heart, I knew my little one*

*had gone to be with you. My body confirmed this to be true
before any other person even suspected it. Yet I was compelled
by some small hope to press forward and not verbalize what
I already knew. Lord, I am experiencing a grief like no other.
I have often heard of women who miscarried their babies,
but I never comprehended their agony. Yet now, so close to
what I'd thought would be delivery, I am facing their pain.
I do not think I can bear up under such tremendous sorrow.
Taking my next breath requires all my effort. And the thought
of explaining this tragedy to my other children is too much
for me. Lord, I cannot conceive of life without my unborn
baby sharing my days. I do not even have the words for this
moment. How should I petition you? My needs are so great
and so numerous that I cannot count them all. Lord, and
you are Lord of all, will you reach me at my lowest point and
lift me up? Bestow upon my loved ones and me your solid
resource of grace and hope. Even now, I feel myself tumbling
lower still. I will not pass through this without your strong
hands of support guiding me each step of the way. Please
undertake for me, because of your good, merciful, and compassionate nature. Amen.*

*He who has heard your prayers in the past will not refuse to
supply your need in the present emergency.*
—ARTHUR W. PINK IN *The Attributes of God*

# 40
## Double the Fun

When Dorothy and Will decided to move in together after their respective spouses passed away, this sister and brother were having the time of their lives. Dorothy, having been a widow for over seven years, had been quite adamant with her grown children after her husband had died. Did Dorothy want to come move in with one of them? "No, I've been settled here for over forty-odd years and the last thing I want is to pick up and add more change to my life," Dorothy had replied. Will, Dorothy's younger brother, had lost his wife to cancer the year before and found his own adjustment difficult at best. He felt so alone rambling around in his own large home without his beloved Sally. After dinner one evening, Dorothy suggested that Will consider selling his place and moving in with her. "We can help each other," she'd said. "I can't keep up with the outside repairs or the yard work, but I still have enough energy to take care of the inside and do all the cooking." Will silently considered Dorothy's offer. He promised to think about it.

Later that evening, Dorothy heard the phone ring, and as soon as she answered it Will asked, "Can I bring my dog?" "Of course," Dorothy replied. "Well then," Will said, "I guess I've thought enough. I'll start making the necessary arrangements right away." Some eight weeks later, Dorothy was directing her great flock of children, grandchildren, nieces, and nephews as they lugged all of Will's belongings into the house. While she pointed out where to place his things, Will was busy outside getting his lawnmower and tools put away in the pole barn. All the while, Dorothy's and Will's kids passed sidelong glances at one another, wondering if their respective parent knew what they were doing. And they did. It wasn't long before both Dorothy and Will settled into a comfortable routine. And did they ever laugh! Right after lunch, they sat at the kitchen table enjoying another cup of coffee and reminiscing about times long past. No one else still remembered these events, so sharing them was good medicine—probably the best medicine of all for folks their age.

*O satisfy us in the morning with Thy loving-kindness,*
*That we may sing for joy and be glad all our days.*
—PSALM 90:14

*Dear Lord, may I simply say thank you for the generous ways in which you provide for me? All these long years you've been so faithful to me. Through good times and bad, you've seen me through. Often I doubted my own strength to see a challenge to its completion, but you were with me, guiding me, holding me up, loving me. Even though I am now old in body, my spirit is rejuvenated day by day. I sense your continued good work in me even now. As I walk nearer and nearer to my life's end, I pray that you will continue to stand close by my side. I understand that as I become weaker and frailer in my physical body, I'll need you all the more. It won't be easy; it isn't always easy now. Yet I cannot deny your hand of provision upon me. Your goodness is evident wherever I look. And during these past months, which could have been so overwhelming, you have graciously given me an extra special time with my loved one. As I share my home with those I love, I am blessed all the more. I am enjoying such sweet communion at a time of life I had never expected such bounty. Especially now, when I've lost so many dear folk to death, my memories are invaluable to me. And to have the opportunity to share and share alike is indeed a wondrous thing. Thank you, Lord, for the answers that come before I even think to pray. You know me inside and out, and you love me still. How can I not praise you for such lavishness? I do so now with a heart filled and overflowing with gratefulness. Amen.*

*How we channel our lives today helps prepare us for the future.*
—CARLA JIVIDEN PEER IN *A Quiet Heart*

# 41
## Sheltered

Connie sat holding the hand of her daughter Meg. Together they rocked slowly on Connie's porch swing overlooking the burgeoning vegetable and flower gardens. As Connie silently pushed her feet off from the roughened planks beneath her feet, she tried to remember the names of the annuals her late sister, Shannon, had been eager to plant this spring. Not having the slightest clue which posies her sister had selected upset Connie. She frowned, planted her feet on the floor, and abruptly got up. "What is it, Mom?" Meg queried gently. "What's upset you?" "Nothing except I'm already forgetting the things Shannon loved most. I'm afraid I might forget her altogether before long." "It'll never happen," Meg said resolutely. "You two were closer than most married people I know. And you've spent the last ten years living together, too. I'd like to know if there is anything at all you don't know about Aunt Shannon?"

She's right, of course, Connie concurred. Shannon and I did enjoy a close relationship. It's just been so still around here since she's been gone. Sometimes I'm frightened that I'll not be able to care for her beloved garden in the way she did. That all she labored for will be lost because of my simple ignorance. Oh why didn't I pay more attention while she was still alive? I was always too busy with my precious vegetables to take the time to learn about her flowers. What was it I always said, that my vegetables pay their own way while flowers end up getting discarded at day's end? Used to make her fuss a bit, Connie acknowledged. But she knew what I meant. She always did. Shannon and I understood each other. We were sensible enough to enjoy each day for whatever it brought our way. And did we ever make mischief, Connie thought with a chuckle. "Now what's on your mind?" Meg asked suspiciously. "I'm just thinking about the time Shannon and I got stuck in the 'recline' position of our electric chairs for the afternoon. Remember when that storm came through and the electricity went out? We were stuck up in midair for over three hours! And Shannon tried to get me to slide my way down to get help. Oh, my," Connie laughed until she cried, "you should have seen the two of us, singing and carrying on like a couple of grade-school girls." Meg tilted her head at her mom's tear stained cheeks, "With antics like that, you were afraid you'd forget Aunt Shannon?"

*But let all who take refuge in Thee be glad,*
*Let them ever sing for joy;*
*And mayest Thou shelter them,*
*That those who love Thy name may exult in Thee.*
—PSALM 5:11

*Dear Lord, what a fool I've been lately. Worrying and fretting about losing my memory. Lord, how do you have the* patience to put up with me? I've been sitting around and stewing these past weeks all because I'm afraid I'll forget my loved one. Silly, isn't it? How could I ever forget the one who's been closer to me this last decade than any other? It's been heavy on my heart, though, that the older I get, the more concentration it takes for me to recall little details. And my dear sister was so into the finer points of life. She loved to take care that everything was just so. Lord, I don't want to let those special qualities that made her unique pass from my heart and mind. I need her to stay close to me.

I never would have thought that I'd struggle so with this inconsequential issue. Yet it matters greatly to me that I continue to honor her memory. And I will. But I also realize that at my age, I'll likely never experience that camaraderie and kinship with another living soul. We had a relationship that went beyond the bonds of sisterhood. We were friends. Best friends. Thank you, Lord, for this precious gift you gave me in her. I am privileged to have shared such sweet communion with one so loving. She was my example in countless ways. I pray that I will continue to bless your name for the time we were allotted. Make me wise, Lord, wise enough to look to you for the grace I require to focus on all the good you've bestowed upon me. Amen.

When you've seen the ordinary enough, you are jarred by the extraordinary.
—CINDY CROSBY IN *By Willoway Brook*

# 42

## Sudden Sorrow

Leah, fifty-one-year-old mother of two and grandmother of four, held the latest request in her hand. Her employer had sent Leah an information sheet on the elderly couple she hoped Leah would consider caring for during the weekday evening hours. Leah hadn't said yes, but she hadn't said no either, so that was a start. With all of her experience as an in-home health care worker, Leah's bailiwick had always been working with geriatric patients. As she began to age herself, Leah's empathic side grew to huge proportions as she started having to face some of the same obstacles as that of her charges. Leah, whose patience rarely wore thin, was just the right medicine for these frail folk who relied on her for more than assistance with simple chores. Whenever Leah entered a home, she wasn't merely a facilitator, she became a friend for life. During her off-duty hours, Leah filled her time grandmothering her four young grandchildren. She frequently went from one end of the caregiving spectrum to the other. Diapering the babies, chasing after toddlers, making a mid-morning snack, Leah was adept at it all. Life for Leah was predictable, but she was contented with that. She expected to continue working until she was no longer physically able, for as Leah would say, there's always someone out there who'll need a hand.

But Leah had never anticipated getting the news that her only grandson had been killed in an accident on the playground. He was rushed to the ER, but never regained consciousness. The head injury had caused massive bleeding, and Tyler was gone. Leah sped to the hospital, but she was too late. Her beloved grandchild had died before she arrived. The ensuing weeks were mere blurs to Leah. She couldn't remember from one day to the next what she was supposed to do. Her children and friends tried to help Leah as they worked through their own grief. And yet Leah felt herself spiraling out of control. She knew she needed to get back to the task of living, for even in her own grief, Leah's natural nurturing instinct began to automatically kick in. She understood how much her family needed her to be well; it would lift at least one weight from their already overburdened hearts. So Leah sat fingering the job description again: a married couple with no immediate family who needed some minor assistance around the house. Well, Leah considered, perhaps taking this job and helping out is exactly the medicine I need.

*I know, O Lord, that Thy judgments are righteous,*
*And that in faithfulness Thou hast afflicted me.*
*O may Thy lovingkindness comfort me,*
*According to Thy word to Thy servant.*
—PSALM 119:75–76

*Dear Lord, I am bereft of consolation. I cannot conceive of any words that would bring comfort to me now. I feel such sorrow, such immense soul pain, that I sometimes think it will consume me. Lord, help me now. Let your Holy Spirit intercede within my heart and plea on my behalf. Will this agony ever abate? Will I ever be whole again? Lord, I cannot envision a time when the memory of my beloved will cease to cause me inexpressible grief. Yet in the midst of this dark night, I see faint glimmers of your goodness from times past. Barely, I perceive that you continue to stretch out your hands of compassion and care toward me. I want to take them into my own. But I am afraid. I am frightened of what may be expected of me as I reenter the world of the living. Staying put, in this place of despair, seems safer to me now. But you are persistent in your pursuit of me. Because of your great love toward me, you will not leave me to my despair. You want me to take comfort in you. You wait for me to embrace life again, to follow you in service. Lord, I cannot do this thing without your constant and immediate intervention. I want to love again, to live again. I do not know the way. Will you show me even now? Will you cleanse me of my wariness and enable me to trust you? Amen.*

*For we will never be able to pick up the basin and towel, or the paintbrush or the ballet slipper, until we have first submitted in humility to the Servant Lord.*
—MICHAEL CARD IN *Scribbling in the Sand*

# PART FIVE

# Forsaken Dreams

Life is full of losses and gains. Whether those losses are due to poor health, financial setbacks, job changes, or relational hurdles, every woman will face a variety of obstacles that stand in direct opposition to her dreams and desires. How we choose to handle these painful experiences will in time serve to define who we become. Eventually, our decision to courageously persist through these periods of trial will serve us well. Any perceived "loss" could transform into even greater gain as we search out the good, even the blessed, hidden within every veiled challenge.

# 43
## Self-Sabotaged

With paper and pen in hand, Jill sat doodling a hangman's noose. After each additional condemning line, she recalled yet another former boyfriend's name. By the time the hangman was dangling over the empty page, Jill had run through the list of over twenty-five years' worth of romances gone sour. *That's it,* Jill thought desperately, *it's clear I'll never find someone to share my life with.* At forty-eight years old, Jill had already given up her dream of becoming a mother. She reconciled that fact three years earlier when she turned forty-five and her body entered menopause. Now, nearing the half-century mark, Jill was lamenting over the demise of her most recent romantic entanglement. And "entanglement" described this nine-month fling to a tee.

Jill had met him through mutual friends. Although she was bound and determined not to go on any blind dates, as usual her friends' persistence had worn her resistance down until Jill had finally relented. After the first date, Jill was flabbergasted. Could it be? Had she actually enjoyed the previous five hours? She was astounded at how comfortable she felt, how much she'd laughed. All in all, Jill and Brad had clicked. Weeks went by and the two grew closer still. Brad began talking marriage. Jill was thrilled beyond measure. One evening they even stopped to peruse the diamonds in shop windows after dinner. Finding one Jill adored, Brad went inside and asked the salesman to hold it for them. Jill recalled going home that evening and pinching herself. Yes, the evening had transpired. And better still, she and Brad had gone shopping for engagement rings. That night, Jill couldn't sleep. Who could? After so many years of waiting, Jill believed Brad was the one. The one she had waited for since her college days were over. She thanked God again and again for His perfect timing and perfect provision.

Less than forty-eight hours later, however, Brad didn't show up for their date to the symphony. He didn't call, didn't return Jill's calls either. After another two weeks of such nonsense, Jill finally tracked Brad down. He confessed he'd met someone else. Now Jill was trying to cope with another dashed dream, and the only one she was certain could help her put her shattered heart back together was God himself.

*Unless the Lord builds the house,*
*They labor in vain who build it.*
—PSALM 127:1A

*Dear Lord, I'm not sure how to reconcile my strong desires for marriage and family with my life as a single person. I believe that you give us these desires for lifelong companionship and that marriage is a good thing. Still, I've been waiting for you to bring someone into my life for many years. Lord, after this last fiasco I'm done with dating. Words cannot fully describe the feelings of rejection and shame I'm experiencing now. It was difficult enough before this last relationship ended so abruptly, but now I have new wounds to tend that just keep festering. Memories of love lost, dreams destroyed, and unrequited commitment overtake me now. I'm in a whirlpool of remembrances that continue to pull me under. I'm trying in vain to push aside the betrayal and keep going, but it's not possible. Everything I do reminds me of him!*

*Help me, Lord. Bring your lasting healing to my hurting heart. Complete me. Let me find my needs for intimacy and companionship within the bounds of my relationship with you. Root out the seeds of self-pity and bitterness that war within me. Unless you cleanse my soul, I cannot go on. My zeal for life has been so undermined by one hurtful relationship after another. Lord, will you put a guard around me? Give me your wisdom to anticipate danger and help me avoid destructive people. Show me how to live and walk in the strength of your spirit all the days of my life. Transform my wounded heart into a triumphant, victorious one. Remake me from the inside out. Mold my perspectives as you see fit. Be the lover of my soul, I pray. Let me recognize your hand of protection and compassion every day of my life. Give me the grace to proclaim this truth and find security in it. Amen.*

*Always call on God before calling a counselor.*
—STORMIE OMARTIAN IN *Lord, I Want to Be Whole*

# 44
## Sacrificial Love

As Angela waited with bated breath for the doctor to finish her examination, she held back the tears. Once she started crying, there would be no stopping. You can do this, Angela commanded herself. Hands clenching the coarse paper covering the table where she lay flat on her back, Angela realized she was ripping it to shreds. OK, you can sit up now, her OB gently instructed. Scooting back, Angela sat up and looked intently into her doctor's eyes; she knew without a word what the diagnosis was. "I'm sorry," her physician said sympathetically. "You were right, Angela, you did lose the baby. It probably happened last night during that bout of cramping you told me about." Angela nodded, she knew of course, but her husband had wanted Angela seen by her doctor just to be sure. At that moment, any vestige of self-control Angela had crumbled into a wake of trembling and tears. "I am sorry," her OB soothed. "You're still young, you can try again later in the year." Nodding again, Angela got up and dressed. She hurried outside through the waiting room and clumsily unlocked the door to her car. Inside, with doors locked, Angela leaned over the steering wheel to weep in earnest.

Why, Lord? Why now? You know what tomorrow is, my only sister's baby shower. And I was going to wait until after the shower to tell Mary the good news. She would have been so thrilled that the two of us could share the excitement of being pregnant at the same time. Of course, I won't even tell her I was pregnant. But what wretched timing this is. I still cannot believe that I've lost my baby. After trying to get pregnant for these past three years only to lose this precious child so quickly, I feel so very grief-stricken. Yet I have to, want to, rejoice with my sister. Help me, Lord, to look past my own pain and share sincerely in my dear sister's happiness during the coming days and weeks.

*My sorrow is beyond healing,*
*My heart is faint within me!*
—JEREMIAH 8:18

*Dear Lord, you are my only hope, my sole comfort, and my single source of strength. It doesn't matter that others near me are trying to bring comfort my way. I cannot receive it. My heart, once so full, is empty, shallow, and bereft of any good thing. I am so far away. It's as though I am drifting along, in my own pain, unable to grasp hold of reason or sense. Lord, I am afraid that my grieving will take over my life. I cannot comprehend the hows or the whys of such a tragic occurrence. And the timing seems too cruel for explanation. Still, in my soul, I know that you are the God who loves me. This doesn't make sense if I only regard the circumstances of my life. But when I look past the pain, I do see glimmers of your love shine through. Extend your hand of mercy to me now. I can scarcely lift my own up to meet yours. I am overcome with sorrow, with pangs of despair so wrenching that I must concentrate on taking my next breath. I do not even know how to pray. What should I ask for? Strength, wisdom, insight? Will any of these choice gifts bring back my child? No. So I am left to resignedly beg for mercy and grace. Bring your healing to me, Lord. I am unable to see the good in this, so you must overshadow my confusion with your redemptive presence. See me as the frail, hopeless woman I now am, and please meet my urgent cries for help as only you can. Swiftly, I pray, come near me and let me experience your joy once again. Amen.*

> *One of the most difficult lessons we must learn in life is that it is often unfair. One of the greatest hopes we have in life is that God has glorious power to make us better and stronger in the midst of life's inequities.*
> —SHARON MARSHALL WITH JEFF JOHNSON IN *Take My Hand*

# 45
## Remembering Us

Sue got up each morning and thanked God for another day, another chance to live. Dutifully, she took a legion of pills at breakfast. Then she got dressed and went out for her two-mile walk. Returning home, she did the chores around the house and ordered her day. Much of Sue's time lately was spent on the Internet or at the library, where she was researching everything she could find on Alzheimer's. Always, always, Sue had been the one fighting both major and minor bouts of illness. She fought her way through countless heart procedures and three subsequent operations. Sue never expected to grow old with her husband, Bob. So sick was she that at one point she had even planned the details of her funeral. Then, almost miraculously, a new specialist came into Sue's life, made a startling diagnosis, and discovered a way to treat Sue's heart condition more effectively. Skeptical at first, Sue and Bob didn't know what to think. How had all these other physicians failed to see what Sue's real problem had been? Slowly, Sue made remarkable progress, overjoyed to become a walking, talking miracle.

At last Sue and Bob could relish their time together as empty nesters, or so they believed. After a recent routine exam, Bob casually mentioned symptoms he was having to his family physician. Tests were ordered, nothing conclusive came back. But Bob continued to decline mentally. He found it difficult to remember, had trouble placing names and faces, and even stopped doing the bills because he couldn't recall if he'd already paid them. Troubled by her spouse's inability to make decisions, Sue pressed the matter with their physician once more. After a closer look, Sue, Bob, and their doctor realized that Bob was in the early stages of Alzheimer's. Sue, the "sick" one, now faced the shocking realization that she would be the one doing the care taking, not her once strong and independent spouse. Instead of crumbling under such a devastating diagnosis, Sue took stock of the situation and put all her newfound energy into trying to keep her Bob as healthy as possible for as long as possible. She knew firsthand that a doctor's grim prognosis doesn't necessary mean the end of life.

*For whoever wishes to save his life shall lose it; but whoever loses his life for My sake shall find it.*
—MATTHEW 16:25

*Dear Lord, you know my struggles, you alone are privy to my deepest fears. All these long years I've believed that death was always just a step ahead of me. I anticipated it even. I knew I would not live to see old age. And I accepted this hard truth. Then a miracle of sorts was brought into my life. Today I am renewed both in body and spirit. I am faced with the possibility of a long and even healthy life. Thank you, Lord, you have done a wonderful thing for me. Yet my heart is in a stranglehold of confusion. I am torn betwixt and between. Help me sort out my feelings. I am so grateful for your healing touch upon my life, but what about my loved one's health? Now I am facing an even greater challenge. I must be the one who is strong enough to endure my dear one's decline. Unless you heal the body of my loved one, it will only be a matter of time before a great chasm of silence comes between us. With no memory, no mental acuity, our relationship as we now know it will change, will die.*

*I understand that there is no going back, nor would I desire to alter the hands of time. Yet I struggle with unknowns about the future. Will I be strong enough to handle all that will come to pass? How can I face tomorrow with the knowledge that I may soon be alone in every sense save the physical? Undertake for me now, Lord. I am so unsure and afraid. Help me remain calm, be wise, and relish each day we still have together. Let not fear overcome the grace you give me today. Enable us both to keep our eyes fixed on you, the author and giver of life. Remind us moment by moment that our lives are in your capable, faithful hands. Amen.*

*Joy and grief are Siamese twins.*
—BRUCE NYGREN IN *Touching the Shadows*

# 46
## Residual Effects

$\mathcal{H}$olly loved a party. She relished planning the food, selecting the décor, even making out the invitations was a delight for her. Since her daughter's eleventh birthday was just three weeks away, Holly was busy mentally tabulating how many guests there would be and where to seat everyone. Finally she decided to sit down and make a written list then and there. She was halfway through the invitations when she came to her parents' names. As Holly swallowed a groan, her countenance fell. This was so hard, Holly thought with resentment. Another repercussion from their divorce fallout that no one ever talks about. Holly had tried to come to terms with her parents' divorce five years earlier. Instead of getting easier, it got tougher to take. Although her parents never, ever made a scene at any of Holly's family gatherings, it was so painful for her to witness her once happily married parents arriving with new spouses in tow. It rankled Holly to no end to see them casually hobnobbing and enjoying one another's company.

What is this, Holly thought with irritation, just a casual get together for the once unhappily marrieds, now happily remarrieds? Ack. Holly's stomach twisted at the thought. If there had been any way to keep them apart just so she wouldn't have to witness such tender scenes, Holly would have done it. But Holly's husband had made it clear immediately following her parents' separation. *We're not holding duplicate birthday and holiday parties just because your folks decided to split up. They made their decision, they have to live with it.* And I suppose I better grow up and get used to it as well, Holly decided. Uncomfortable or not, Holly looked ahead and realized she would play hostess to not only her own parents but their new spouses as well, so she tried to make the best of it.

*Do not be grieved, for the joy of the Lord is your strength.*
—Nehemiah 8:10b

*Dear Lord, can you help me make sense of this troublesome situation? I feel like my own emotions are chaotic at best. Every which way I am compelled to play the congenial daughter, the one who must simply smile and pretend everything is just fine. Lord, you know it is not so. My parents have made a decision that brings pain and regret to our entire family. It is not my place to judge, yet I fight the temptation to unleash my anger on the both of them. I am so disappointed that my own children won't grow up in the knowledge and security of grandparents who love each other as well as them. I want life back the way it was when I was young. I admit to feeling resentment toward them both. Lord, I realize that each of us is accountable for our own decisions; our choices are ours alone. Yet I struggle mightily with wanting to warn them off by informing them how much hurt they've brought on us all. A part of me needs for them to realize that their choice has sent repercussions throughout our family. And I see that it will never change; their decision will always force us into accommodating their new status as independent remarried couples.*

*Lord, I need your touch of grace today. I am sorely tried and tempted to rehash, time and again, all that I've sacrificed as well. I pray that their decision will not have a negative impact on my family. Help my dear children see that commitment, through the good times and the bad, is worth the effort. Let them not be swayed by the mistakes of others who might whisper tempting thoughts to give up when there is still opportunity for healing and reparation. Please keep my family strong and close to your heart of hearts, Lord. Make a way for us through this distressing time of throwaway relationships and cast-off vows. I ask that you would place a hedge around us all. Let our mutual love for one another seep into the hearts of those we care for most. May your unconditional love abound yet even more. Amen.*

*It is good to remember that the tea kettle, although up to its neck in hot water, continues to sing.*
—*God's Little Devotional Journal for Women*

# 47
## Checkmate

When Lynn arrived at her workplace Tuesday morning after returning from a buying convention, she was exhausted but still eager to show her manager what she'd purchased for the fall line. Prior to her trip, Lynn had taken great care to research her small retail company's past year's sales. She had proven time and again that she knew how to predict what would sell best for any special event or holiday, and she prepared exhaustively for each sales show she attended. With the rigors of traveling behind her and a successful season approaching, Lynn couldn't help but think about the carrot her boss had dangled in front of her right before she left the previous week. Lynn had replayed that conversation in her mind's eye until she was able to reproduce it with minimal effort. She was more hopeful now than ever before that this verbal promise would materialize into the long-awaited promotion she'd been coveting for the last three years. Come one-thirty, I'm in that office, Lynn decided. After I make my short presentation, I'll ask for more details. One way or another, I'd really like to get a firm commitment sometime today.

After trying to catch up on a week's worth of voice mail, e-mail, faxes, and in-house requests, Lynn's morning flew by. Before she knew it, a coworker peeked into her office and invited Lynn to lunch. "Gladly," Lynn said thankfully. Anything to get through the next hour, she thought to herself. Once lunch break was over, Lynn glanced at her watch, almost one-thirty, and was on her way. After a simple presentation of the goods she'd ordered, Lynn cut to the chase and invited more information regarding her promotion by making reference to their pre-trip conversation. Lynn was sharp; it didn't take but a few minutes for her to realize that she had been passed by again. Why? Lynn wanted to know. Walking back to her own office, all she could remember was some lame excuse that included that tired phrase, "circumstances beyond my control." Well, if I can't be promoted from within, maybe it's time I started looking outside.

*But refuse foolish and ignorant speculations, knowing that they produce quarrels. And the Lord's bond-servant must not be quarrelsome, but be kind to all, able to teach, patient when wronged.*
—2 TIMOTHY 2:23–24

*Dear Lord, how can this nightmare be happening to me? I have worked long, hard hours to get to this place, where I was promised recompense for my labor. And now, it has been stripped away for no good reason. Lord, I am so angry. I want nothing more than to verbally unleash my frustrations on the person who has wronged me. It is not as though I went chasing after an elusive, frivolous object. Rather, I have sacrificed to make myself ready and qualified for such a position. Yet even when promised this rare opportunity, I have been jilted and passed over—again. I do not understand. None of this makes any sense to me. Lord, what should I do? Please extend your wisdom to me. I am contemplating leaving, maybe starting over somewhere else. Is this wrong of me? Am I quitting before I see this issue through? I am not sure. All I really know is that I am disappointed and a bit disillusioned. I am trying to make all the pieces fit together and yet I do not have the facts to do so. Help me think this through clearly. Give me your insight and wisdom as I attempt to make the best choices for my life. Lord, please enable me to represent you in a way that brings honor to your name. Despite my personal struggles, I never want to abandon self-control and allow my desire for retribution to bring dishonor to you. Help me now. Mend my brokenness with your compassion and constant care. I bring my shattered dreams, once again, before your throne, knowing that this isn't the end of my life's story. Amen.*

*There is something about heaven and eternity that we have to grasp, because if we don't, we'll miss everything else. We'll read the music but never sing, study the choreography but never dance. It's this: Heaven starts now.*
—MARK BUCHANAN IN *Things Unseen*

# 48

## Empty Arms

*W*hen Deana hung up the telephone she wanted to cry, but she didn't. Instead of tears, an emptiness deep inside welled up and consumed any flow of tears she might have shed. Deana's sadness and regret washed over her again. "If onlys" crept through her mind only to accuse her of repeated failures and past mistakes. It was a pattern she had tried to break, but no matter how hard she tried, anytime a new challenge presented itself, Deana wondered if her choices from years ago were coming back to haunt her now. Trying to shake herself free of the pit of despair she was currently spiraling into, Deana feebly reminded herself that her daughter was an adult now. Carrie must decide for herself.

True enough, Deana's marriage to Carrie's father had been short-lived and turbulent, but Deana had rallied once the divorce was final and had done the best job she could as a single mom. Even so, Carrie frequently reminded Deana that she would never, ever bring a child into the world only to expose it to the deprivations she had experienced. No matter that Deana reminded Carrie that she had a terrific, committed husband to parent any children right alongside of her, Carrie turned a deaf ear to her mom and often retorted with a stinging comeback. "Isn't that what you thought when you married Dad and had me?" Deana had winced. There weren't any guarantees in life. But to miss out on parenting because of anger or bitterness was pathetic. Deana had hoped and prayed throughout Carrie's growing up years that her daughter wouldn't be scarred by the difficulties they had faced. These days, Deana realized that she needed to step up her own private commitment to continue praying earnestly for her daughter's ability to let go and forgive, just as she had many years earlier.

*To Thee, O Lord, I lift up my soul.*
*O my God, in Thee I trust,*
*Do not let me be ashamed;*
*Do not let my enemies exult over me.*
—PSALM 25:1–2

*Dear Lord, I am so full of regret and remorse. I am unable to forget the choices I made so many long years ago. Even on the infrequent days when I am able to see past my mistakes, I'm all too quickly reminded of the painful repercussions of my decisions. My own daughter, with her lingering resentment, brings such agony to my heart. Lord, I want to be free. I do not want to live my life always looking back over my shoulder, despairing over what might have been. This is my life. For better or worse, I must handle whatever comes my way. Will you give me the strength and grace to face this obstacle with a calmness so foreign to me? I need your provision to make it through this day, even this very hour. My soul feels as though it is constantly being torn apart. I do understand why resentment and bitterness have taken root in the heart of this one I love. But is there no way to get past the hurt? Is there hope for reconciliation, for genuine healing? I pray it is so. Lord, if there is any offensive attitude within me, please remove it. Take away anything that might cause a wedge between my loved one and myself. And Lord, will you do a work of heart cleansing in us all? Help my family to embrace their own future with a strong, vibrant faith inspired by your faithfulness. Let them live their lives with a courageous determination to do what is right in your eyes alone. Please strengthen them with your presence and give them all they require to put the past to rest. I pray that forgiveness will abound and a spirit of generosity and mercy will encircle my family. Lord, be with us now. Be our instructor and guide through these volatile emotions. Lead us home to you and to the safety of your perfect love. Amen.*

> *It's true—as Christians, eternal life is ours. But the choice to live free in spirit as "immortals" or as unhappy children of earth is also ours.*
> —GRACE KETTERMAN AND DAVID HAZARD IN *When You Can't Say "I Forgive You"*

# 49
## Motion Detector

Ann Marie's monthly travel magazines had arrived, and once again she was consumed by wanderlust. As she perused the glossy color photos of faraway places, Ann Marie felt a catch in her throat. Of all times, why now, Lord? Ann Marie couldn't believe she was caught in the midst of a merger. She didn't know whether she would even have a job in four months. Like the rest of the middle managers, Ann Marie had been called into a meeting just days earlier. They had all heard the rumors, but Ann Marie didn't believe them. Every now and again, the gossip mill did its work too exuberantly and Ann Marie made it a policy to not take stock of every little breath of "news."

Still, after that two-hour stretch of questions and answers, Ann Marie's head came out spinning. She didn't want to lose her job; she was comfortable and content. At fifty-plus years, Ann Marie's last wish was to go out hunting for another position. Add her long-anticipated trip to New Zealand to the mix, and Ann Marie felt devastated. I've saved and scrimped for over five years to be able to afford this once-in-a-lifetime trip and now I'm faced with having to consider calling it off. It's been a long, hard road for me to get this close to realizing my dream of traveling overseas. I won't give in to fear of the unknown just because

of job instability. What am I, crazy? Ann Marie reconsid-
ered. I do have to consider my financial future too. I may
be unemployed before I even board the plane. Ann Marie
closed her magazine and tossed it aside. She felt as though
every time she inched nearer to her dream of traveling to
distant lands, unseen hands ripped it away, again leaving
Ann Marie bereft and befuddled. Not this time, Ann Marie
determined. I'll make my plans as wisely as possible, but by
faith I'll be on that plane come departure time.

*Thou dost open Thy hand,*
*And dost satisfy the desire of every living thing.*
—PSALM 145:16

*Dear Lord, here I am again: ready, eager, and willing to go*
*on an adventure. But that just never seems to be my lot in*
*life. I can understand how desires and dreams must be tem-*
*porarily deferred at times. Life is too untamable to make*
*plans with 100 percent certainty. Yet I do wonder why I have*
*this lifelong desire of wanting to see and experience more of*
*the world you've created but am thwarted at every turn. This*
*makes no sense. And I also recognize that life happens. It just*
*feels as though "life happens" to me more than to most. I do*
*not mean to complain or to ramble on about my losses. True*
*enough, they are neither momentous nor life threatening.*
*But it still rankles that after all my careful, prudent living,*
*I am to be put off yet again. Lord, I ask you now to do a*

*great work of heart cleansing within my soul. Remake me
into a woman who's solely content with your abiding love.
I have lived long enough to know that you alone can supply
and satisfy my deepest longings. No person, no event, no
possession can bring the inner peace and fulfillment I crave.
Lord, you know me inside and out. You have created me
with certain gifts, bents, and aptitudes. I give them to you to
use as you see fit. May my deepest heart's longing be pleasing
in your sight. Give me, I pray, all that I require to bring
goodness and glory to your name. Teach me to trust you as a
child would. Embrace me now, in my disappointment and
pain, and shore me up to face another day. Let my wounded
soul come to you for the healing touch I need. I will deliber-
ately and with confidence place my desires and dreams into
your faithful hands once again. I pray I might live this life
free of want because of all that you have already given me
through your son, Jesus. Amen.*

*Adventure starts in the mind, then travels to the heart.*
—Luci Swindoll in *I Married Adventure*

# 50
# *Above Board*

**W**hen Hannah received the news that her younger sister had finally made partner in the law firm where she'd worked for over ten years, Hannah admittedly squelched feelings of jealousy. Little sister Susan always seemed to get what she wanted, Hannah groused. Hannah could recall countless events during their childhood and adolescent years when Susan offhandedly made comments at the dinner table about obtaining her next conquest. Long after the rest of the family dismissed Susan's chattering as nothing more than pie-in-the-sky pipe dreams, Hannah would stew over every word, expecting Susan to get what she wanted. And Susan did. Not that Susan didn't work for what she wanted; Hannah recognized that Susan had more than her fair share of talent. What Hannah never did figure out was how effortlessly Susan could appear to latch on to a coveted position, possession, or relationship, but once she laid claim to it, it became hers. Unlike her younger sibling, Hannah sacrificed for every high mark in school. She fretted over comparisons made between herself and her sister. Life, it seemed, had handed her the leftovers from Susan's bounty.

As Hannah continued to reminisce over the past and its bitter disappointments, she suddenly felt shell-shocked with Susan's good news. Her own success as a department store manager seemed so inconsequential when compared to Susan's achievements, which were lauded as singularly impressive by one and all. Why, Hannah wondered, was Susan always the shining star and she the flickering candle? Hannah's question of *why* turned to a bigger one of *how* when she realized with dismay that Susan's promotion called for a celebration dinner. Just how will I muster up the strength to smile and offer congratulations that are both heartfelt and sincere? Great, Hannah complained, I have exactly forty-eight hours to get my act together both inside and out. A big job considering just how long I've been rehashing grievances from years past. No time like the present, I suppose, to do some internal inventory and toss out what's been cluttering up my heart and mind for so long— too long.

*With good will render service, as to the Lord, and not to men, knowing that whatever good thing each one does, this he will receive back from the Lord, whether slave or free.*
—EPHESIANS 6:7–8

*Dear Lord, it is a wonder to me that so many seasons have passed and still I continue to hold onto old hurts, wounds, and scars. It amazes me still more that I believe I am right in my stance. I understand that everyone has been given particular gifts and talents, and that we must use whatever resources* we have to the fullest potential. Why then, do I grumble against what another has? Am I so very small minded that I resent what I do not possess? I am ashamed to admit that for far too long I have nurtured a hateful, resentful mindset. Please forgive me. I really cannot explain why it has taken me so long to see that I've been the one who is wrong. No one else has intentionally hurt me. In fact, my loved ones have gone the extra distance time and again to help me feel loved and accepted. It has been my own blind bitterness that has erected a wall of distrust between us. Help me now, Lord, to seek forgiveness from those I've wounded. Give me your grace as I attempt to repair the damage inflicted over these many years. Also, enable me to be patient as I seek to build bridges with those I love. Understandably, they may need time to work through their forgiveness toward me. Envelop me in a blanket of your humility and stay near me as I begin this momentous task of realigning my thinking according to biblical truth. I am one needy woman, and I freely admit it. But I put my hope and trust in you for a better today, a brighter, more joyful tomorrow. Lord, all that I am, I give to you. My desires, my dreams, every part of me, I commit once again into your keeping. Open my eyes and let me see beyond this temporal and transient existence. Let me see you, Lord. Amen.

> Importunate prayer is not a sign of pride. It is a sign that our pride is dust. Importunity turns our souls inside out. We learn what we really think as the Spirit dredges deep.
> —DAVID HANSEN IN *Long Wandering Prayer*

# 51
## Double Whammy

Victoria hurriedly drove to her gynecologist's office. Today was a big day for her. Although she anticipated hearing the news that her body had already started menopause, Victoria didn't really care anymore. She had long given up on the idea of conceiving her own child. After fifteen years of marriage, countless fertility procedures, and endless tears, Victoria was more than ready to put that dream to rest. Still, her physician wanted to see Victoria just to go over the results from the blood test and answer any questions Victoria might have as her body entered menopause. Let's get this meeting over with, Victoria thought impatiently. So she wove in and out of traffic, trying to reach the office as soon as possible. "This won't take too long, thankfully," Victoria said aloud, "because I've got more important tasks to tie up today."

Today. The long-awaited day in May when her lawyer had scheduled a meeting to sign the last of the papers so that Victoria and her husband would become the legal parents of their foster son, Connor. Victoria couldn't wait. After she scooted Connor off to school that morning and sent her spouse to work, she labored over what to wear. Finally, Victoria decided upon a casual suit. She was anxious to put one painful life experience behind her as she opened the door to a much more satisfying one. Can it be that we've had Connor for over three years? She had wondered back then if she was cut out of stern enough stuff to handle a then five-year-old boy with a boatload of anger and distrust. But hadn't they hung in there, overcome the obstacles, and finally learned to live and love as a family? Yes! Victoria could hardly wait to reach deep into her purse and pull out that magnificent Monte Blanc pen, the one she purchased expressly for this commemorative event. Entering the parking garage, Victoria grabbed her bag and opened her door when her cell phone rang. Curious, Victoria thought as she answered the call. "No!" Victoria moaned, "it couldn't be. Another delay? Why? What? Connor's birth father has second thoughts now? He hasn't even seen Connor in over two years. We'll reschedule next month?" Pressing the end button, Victoria abjectly sat back in her car and closed her eyes, trying to decide what she was going to tell her son Connor that evening at dinner. Taking a deep breath, Victoria prayed an urgent, silent prayer: Lord, give me the faith and the confidence I need to overcome this setback for the sake of my family. I'm counting on you.

*He makes the barren woman abide in the house*
*As a joyful mother of children.*
*Praise the Lord!*
   —PSALM 113:9

*Dear Lord, is this really happening? Am I dreaming? Is there some huge cosmic joke being played on me? I wonder, because it certainly feels that way. I am unable to process this information. I cannot believe that another setback has occurred. Lord, haven't we suffered enough? Haven't I, personally, been through more than my share of disappointments and pain in the parenting department? Why is this happening again? Finally, I thought it was over, that we would have our child, legally, at last. Now another glitch has arisen and we're left loving a child that could possibly be taken from us at any time. Lord, please help me make sense of this situation. Enable me to work this through so that I am able to continue on. I am so very tempted to shut down emotionally again. I simply want to withdraw. This just hurts too much. How do I dare to open my wounds and brave being torn apart? Lord, you alone can help me overcome my natural tendencies to pull back. I know that I must step forth in faith and continue to love my husband and child, but I am afraid. I do not believe I could maintain my sanity if either one were snatched away from me. Bless me now with your abiding presence. Give me a greater portion of your peace than I have ever known before. Meet me, Lord, at my point of need. Help me gain a solid footing and bestow your joy on me as I seek to work through this nightmare once again. Amen.*

*Right thinking brings the peace of God. Right thinking combined with right actions brings the God of peace.*
—RICHARD L. GANZ IN *The Secret of Self-Control*

# 52

## *Loose Change*

Adrienne sat huddled over her desk silently reviewing the bills that needed paying. She emitted a sigh so loud that her dog perked up from across the room and looked expectantly at her. "Don't look at me that way. I've got nothing to give you," Adrienne snapped as she found herself mentally resenting the cost of dry dog food purchased for her family's canine counterpart. Rifling through the seven or so due bills, Adrienne felt like grabbing the entire stack and tossing it into the fireplace. She'd light a match and poof! Their troubles would disappear. If only it were that simple, she lamented. OK, one more time, Adrienne decided, I've got to sort these in order of importance. What needs to be paid first? As Adrienne refiled the bills, crunched some numbers, and made occasional glances up at her wall calendar, she realized with relief that they did have enough in their checking account to cover all the current expenses. Thank God!

After making out the checks and cleaning up the desk area, Adrienne decided she needed a cup of espresso after such a grueling hour. In the kitchen, Adrienne began to unwind as the rich aroma of coffee filled the air. Cupping the drink in her hands, she took a few moments to look over the current family schedule that was slapped on the front of the refrigerator. Adrienne noticed that her children had signed up to attend a football game and tailgate party with their youth group at $10 per child. Her eldest marked a friend's sixteenth birthday party, money for a gift required. Adrienne's son was joining a local Boy Scout troop, registration fees due on Friday. Last, Adrienne's husband needed cash for the dry cleaner's and a departmental donation for a business associate's upcoming wedding. As the caffeine hit Adrienne's system, she felt energized, ready to go, but after summing up the expenses she hadn't counted on, Adrienne's surge of power suddenly turned into a rush of anxiety. Where will we get the money for all these extras, she despaired. OK, pooch, let's go back to the desk one more time and see what we find.

*O Lord, my heart is not proud, nor my eyes haughty;*
*Nor do I involve myself in great matters,*
*Or in things too difficult for me.*
*Surely I have composed and quieted my soul;*
*Like a weaned child rests against his mother,*
*My soul is like a weaned child within me.*
—PSALM 131:1–2

*Dear Lord, I want to cry. I simply cannot continue facing this shortage forever. You know how diligently I try to keep our expenses down. I scrimp and save for the best prices around. I work hard to maintain the material goods we now* possess. Yet for all my labor, we frequently deplete our monthly resources. What else can I do? Will you show me some area where I haven't yet exhausted every avenue to earn new savings? Help me to not lose heart as I manage our funds week by week. Lord, I feel overwhelmed by the rising cost of living. In almost every area, it seems as though prices continue to spike higher yet. And now, my family's needs are in danger of not being met. I hate to see this happen. My mother's heart longs to give them all they ask of me. And the truth is, they do not ask for much. Yet even basics are difficult to supply anymore. Lord, help me continue trusting in your promised provision. I have to admit, we have never once gone without food, clothing, and shelter. But my faith is so weak, I seem to forget who is in charge. I neglect to spend time with you building up my reservoir of faith, wisdom, and truth. Instead, I flutter around nervously, agitated because I can't control my circumstances. I confess that I often give in to "what ifs." Please help me overcome my negativity. Give me your perspective, Lord. Help me set an example for my family in this troublesome financial area. Right now, I hand over this burden. Take it from my wearied shoulders and lift my eyes above that which I cannot change. Instead, let godliness and contentment cover me. Amen.

God's provision is based on unconditional love—not on my faithfulness.
—CECIL MURPHY IN *Seeking God's Hidden Face*

# Sources

## Part One: Too Much to Handle

1 *God's Little Devotional Journal for Women* (Tulsa, Okla.: Honor Books, 2000), p. 360.

2 Richard L. Ganz, *The Secret of Self-Control* (Wheaton, Ill.: Crossway Books, 1998), pp. 163–164.

3 Jud Wilhite, *Faith That Goes the Distance* (Grand Rapids, Mich.: Baker Books, 2002), pp. 88–89.

4 Barbara Johnson, *Look Who's Laughing!* (Grand Rapids, Mich.: Zondervan, 2003), p. 72.

5 John MacArthur, *Twelve Ordinary Men* (Nashville, Tenn.: W Publishing Group, 2002), p. 47.

6 David Hazard, *Reducing Stress* (Eugene, Ore.: Harvest House, 2002), p. 58.

7 Philip Gulley, *Front Porch Tales* (Sisters, Ore.: Multnomah, 1997), p. 150.

8 James Emery White, *Life-Defining Moments* (Colorado Springs, Colo.: WaterBrook Press, 2001), p. 110.

9 Richard J. Foster, *Celebration of Discipline* (San Francisco: HarperSanFrancisco, 1978), p. 30.

10 Max Lucado, *Traveling Light for Mothers* (Nashville, Tenn.: W Publishing Group, 2002), p. 69.

11 Charles R. Swindoll, *Making the Weak Family Strong* (Sisters, Ore.: Multnomah, 1990), p. 55.

12 Cindy Crosby, *By Willoway Brook* (Brewster, Mass.: Paraclete Press, 2003), p. 144.

## Part Two: Relational Setbacks

13 Parker J. Palmer, *Let Your Life Speak* (San Francisco: Jossey-Bass, 2000), p. 96.

14  Calvin Miller, *Jesus Loves Me* (New York: Warner Books, 2002), p. 201.

15  James Emery White, *Long Night's Journey into Day* (Colorado Springs, Colo.: WaterBrook Press, 2002), p. 139.

16  Sheila Walsh, *Living Fearlessly* (Grand Rapids, Mich.: Zondervan, 2000), p. 66.

17  David Hansen, *Long Wandering Prayer* (Downers Grove, Ill.: InterVarsity Press, 2001), p. 31.

18  Jan Silvious, *Look at It This Way* (Colorado Springs, Colo.: WaterBrook Press, 2003), p. 92.

19  Jay E. Adams, *How to Overcome Evil* (Phillipsburg, N.J.: P & R Publishing, 1977), p. 41.

20  Oswald Chambers, *My Utmost for His Highest* (Grand Rapids, Mich.: Discovery House, 1992), Nov. 21.

21  Michael Phillips, *Make Me like Jesus* (Colorado Springs, Colo.: WaterBrook Press, 2003), p. 30.

22  *God's Little Devotional Journal for Women* (Tulsa, Okla.: Honor Books, 2000), p. 337.

## Part Three: In Sickness and Health

23  Sharon Marshall with Jeff Johnson, *Take My Hand* (Grand Rapids, Mich.: Zondervan, 2001), p. 160.

24  Andy Andrews, *The Traveler's Gift* (Nashville, Tenn.: Nelson, 2002), pp. 109–110.

25  Paul David Tripp, *War of Words* (Phillipsburg, N.J.: P & R Publishing, 2000), p. 94.

26  Michael Phillips, *Make Me like Jesus* (Colorado Springs, Colo.: WaterBrook Press, 2003), p. 84.

27  John Sloan, *The Barnabas Way* (Colorado Springs, Colo.: WaterBrook Press, 2002), p. 12.

28  Charles R. Swindoll, *Stress Fractures* (Sisters, Ore.: Multnomah, 1990), p. 222.

29  Jeannie St. John Taylor, *How to Be a Praying Mom* (Peabody, Mass.: Hendrickson, 2001), p. 30.

30  H. Jackson Brown Jr. and Rosemary C. Brown, *Life's Little Instructions from the Bible* (Nashville, Tenn.: Rutledge Hill Press, 2000), p. 147.

31  Jeromy Deibler, *Far from Home* (West Monroe, La.: Howard Publishing, 2001), pp. 118–119.

32  John White, *The Fight* (Downers Grove, Ill.: InterVarsity Press, 1978), p. 97.

## *Part Four: The Final Separation*

33  Larry Crabb, *Finding God* (Grand Rapids, Mich.: Zondervan, 1993), p. 116.

34  Gary Smalley with Al Janssen, *Joy That Lasts* (Grand Rapids, Mich.: Zondervan, 1988), p. 141.

35  Susan Wilkinson, *Getting Past Your Past* (Sisters, Ore.: Multnomah, 2000), pp. 137–138.

36  Sheldon Vanauken, *A Severe Mercy* (New York: Bantam Books, 1979), p. 220.

37  Ann Kroeker, *The Contemplative Mom* (Colorado Springs, Colo.: Shaw, 2000), p. 162.

38  Anne Graham Lotz, *Just Give Me Jesus* (Nashville, Tenn.: W Publishing Group, 2000), p. 148.

39  Arthur W. Pink, *The Attributes of God* (Grand Rapids, Mich.: Baker Book House, 1975), p. 56.

40  Carla Jividen Peer, *A Quiet Heart* (Palos Heights, Ill.: Leadership Resources International, 1998), p. 154.

41  Cindy Crosby, *By Willoway Brook* (Brewster, Mass.: Paraclete Press, 2003), p. 13.

42  Michael Card, *Scribbling in the Sand* (Downers Grove, Ill.: InterVarsity Press, 2002), p. 86.

## *Part Five: Forsaken Dreams*

43  Stormie Omartian, *Lord, I Want to Be Whole* (Nashville, Tenn.: Nelson, 2000), p. 100.

44 Sharon Marshall with Jeff Johnson, *Take My Hand* (Grand Rapids, Mich.: Zondervan, 2001), p. 69.

45 Bruce Nygren, *Touching the Shadows* (Nashville, Tenn.: Nelson, 2000), p. 64.

46 *God's Little Devotional Journal for Women* (Tulsa, Okla.: Honor Books, 2000), p. 301.

47 Mark Buchanan, *Things Unseen* (Sisters, Ore.: Multnomah, 2002), p. 72.

48 Grace Ketterman and David Hazard, *When You Can't Say "I Forgive You"* (Colorado Springs, Colo.: NavPress, 2000), p. 139.

49 Luci Swindoll, *I Married Adventure* (Nashville, Tenn.: W Publishing Group, 2003), p. 29.

50 David Hansen, *Long Wandering Prayer* (Downers Grove, Ill.: InterVarsity Press, 2001), p. 100.

51 Richard L. Ganz, *The Secret of Self-Control* (Wheaton, Ill.: Crossway Books, 1998), p. 164.

52 Cecil Murphy, *Seeking God's Hidden Face* (Downers Grove, Ill.: InterVarsity Press, 2001), p. 110.

# The Author

Michele Howe lives in LaSalle, Michigan, with her husband and four children, whom she has been homeschooling for thirteen years. She is a book reviewer for *Publishers Weekly, CBA Marketplace,* and *CCM Magazine.* Michele has published over seven hundred articles and reviews and is the author of several books, including *Going It Alone: Meeting the Challenges of Being a Single Mom, Pilgrim Prayers for Single Mothers, Prayers to Nourish a Woman's Heart, Prayers for Homeschool Moms,* and *Successful Single Moms.*

### Prayers for Homeschool Moms

Michele Howe

$12.95 Hardcover

ISBN: 0-7879-6557-X

"Michele Howe presents realistic struggles and scenarios home educators can relate to all too well, then takes them by the hand and leads them to the ideal response: intimate dialogue with Jesus. Prepare to be challenged, convicted, comforted, even contemplative, as you pray the prayers of a homeschool mom."

> —**Ann Kroeker**, author of *The Contemplative Mom: Restoring Rich Relationship with God in the Midst of Motherhood*

"Amazingly, Howe addresses every single issue that confronts homeschooling mothers today: each apprehension and thrill, each struggle and triumph. There is a prayer for all of us in this book."

> —**Kristyn Komarnicki**, editor, *PRISM Magazine* and homeschooling mother of three boys

"Michele Howe has not left one stone unturned in this vast compilation of life stories and prayers from moms in the homeschooling community. In *Prayers for Homeschool Moms,* Mrs. Howe guides us from the surface tensions of our lives into the inner sanctum of prayer and hope, reminding us that we are never alone."

> —**Susan Card**, author of *The Homeschool Journey*

This wonderful gift book provides emotional support for those who are balancing the multiple pressures of being a good mom, a good teacher, and a good wife, all from the heart of one seasoned homeschool mom to another. For the mom who is often so overwhelmed by her circumstances that she can't think straight, this book provides welcomed relief, inspiration, and hope through its "teaching" stories—stories that show the inspiring successes of other homeschoolers.

**Michele Howe** is a book reviewer for *Publishers Weekly, CBA Marketplace*, and *CCM Magazine*. Michele has published over 700 articles and reviews and is the author of several books including *Prayers to Nourish a Woman's Heart* and *Prayers of Comfort and Strength*. She lives with her husband and children near LaSalle, Michigan.
[Price subject to change]